Gambia

Travel and Tourism

Travel guide, touristic information, Locations and sights.

Author – Emmanuel Alvin

Published
By
Alvinston Publishing

Createspace Edition

License Note

The entirety of this book is protected as copyright content, under which it is been published and distributed through authorized sources. Your interest to this book is understood to be for self-use, any intention to redistribute it (by any means), digitally or physically is illegal and considered as violation of copyright law. Your access to this book is strictly limited to the authorized distributor or retailer of this book, (in any of its format). It is in accordance with the above conditions that you are allowed to obtain a copy by purchasing it from the legal source that you got it discovered. By acknowledging to these rights are the only means to maintain a relationship with author, publisher and consumer, and promote the advancement of this profession. Certainly there are awareness of the decree that guides the law as punishable (when violated) in every country.

Author Note

Art and Culture on **Gambia**, is intended for the following value; Educational purposes, Touristic information, Business engagements, Holiday intensive and Self-educational purpose. We intend to create awareness to people's interest on African Nations, the effort that we have made in making this project a reality is based on peoples interested areas on African environment, and we are satisfied with what we have done so far. The book pages may not be that long, if you had expected more pages, but that is not our intention, and it does not make the value of a book after-all, but providing you with a book that drives towards your need and provide you the information that make you go for it, and eventually serve you to satisfaction. **Gambia Travel and Tourism** information book will surely get you through.

Note! There is no image in this book, the reason for not including images is to attract a full concentration for better understanding of this book, images are just picture reference, the real attraction is the quality of the book base on the written content. Please go through our Table of Content to see the information headlines, doing so will help you make a choice, and eventually lead you through the part that you need most. Thank you.

Table of Content

Introduction 1
Gambia Travel and Culture 4
   Gambia Cultural Heritage and Tourism 4
   Monuments and Sites 10
   Literature (and Publishing) 30
   Music 35
   Theatre (Drama & Dance) 41
   Fashion and Beauty Pageant 43
   Film 47
Travel to and within Gambia 51
   Travel to Banjul 51
   Travel to Bakau 66
   Travel to Bijilo 74
   Travel to Brufut 78
   Travel to Cape Point 83
   Travel to Fajara 89
   Travel to Gunjur 99
   Travel to Jinack Island 107
   Travel to Kartong 114
   Travel to Kololi 123
   Travel to Kotu 136
   Travel to Makasutu 145
   Travel to Sanyang 156
   Travel to Serrekunda 163
   Travel to Tanji Village 173
Art and Culture 181

Introduction

It is all about African Culture, Art Ethnic group, Tradition, Environment, Religion, People and Custom. A continent of fifty-four independent Nations, when we talk about Africa, we talk about two different race within it, which consists of Arab Africans and black Africans. With the existence of these two race with multi culture and tradition within the continent, Africa would have a lot to offer. Africa is very rich in culture, and tradition is the first priority of every true African. A respected African in his environment must embrace his culture and tradition, this is where the recognition comes from. Africans are preserved with variety of creations and nature that makes up their living, from national resources to mineral resources, wildlife and more. Find out how Africans are coping with the present world, the adaptation and fitting

Originally, the power of an African man is his generations, an African man does his things by faith of his generation and ancestors, what does that mean to you? He should be empowered by what his father left for him, (The wood statue that interprets variety of believes, Elephant tail, that interprets respect, honor, right and title, etc., name them!) in whatever activities he engages in, this makes his force and provide his success, he don't forget to consult the gods of his ancestors when going out This is a typical African man, but how is civilization changing an African man?

Finding out about the entire African environment and its nature, is about knowing the original attitude of human by his origin. The science doesn't tell you everything about our nature but when finding out yourself about us "Human" you will be brought closer to what we were and what we are today. It is amazing to know how an African does his things by his culture from different environment of the continent. A rich cultured African is typical and reserved. He does his things from two or three different information sources, what his mind tells him, what people tell him, and what his ancestors and gods want him to do. How much is an African man keeping fit on his culture and tradition at this present world and its civilization?

In this book you are informed about **Gambia** and its environmental situation related to; Culture, Art, tradition, People, History, Education, Religion, Ethnic group, and more. This book is best used for tourism, Educational purposes, and information on human civilization. Discover Africa and find out what Africa has to offer in all area of life. Information on African country is about knowing our world and how it all came up.

Author - Emmanuel Alvin

Gambia Travel and Culture

Gambia Cultural Heritage and Tourism

A brief history

The RDD started life as the Cultural Archives and ultimately begot what is now known as the NCAC and its various departments. The cultural archives was established in 1971 as a branch of the Public Records Office under the Office of the President of the Gambia with Bakary Sidibeh as its first Research Officer with the special responsibility of collecting both oral traditions and material items of culture for the beginning of a Gambia National Museum.

This was a time when there was growing recognition of the values of oral literature and music by scholars abroad. Gambians realised almost too late that our traditional culture was rapidly changing. For example, the art of the *Griot* was seriously

4

threatened. *Griots* began to lose interest in reciting history and turned more and more to entertainment. Village elders and storytellers were finding fewer young people interested and having time to listen to them. Old people are not like books which can be stored for generations without too much harm, waiting until someone can get round to read them. Traditional ceremonies, songs, cultural games and dances were being abandoned. The growing trend of democracy was weakening class lines and the caste system, undermining the traditional role of craftsmen such as weavers, smiths, leatherworkers, etc. just as was the competition for machine manufactured goods. Most of the masters of music, traditions and handicrafts were aged, between 50-70, and few young men were around to take their places. Since most of our knowledge is transmitted verbally and by demonstration, when these masters were no longer around, their knowledge would die with them.

This awareness led to a desire among some Gambians, to preserve for posterity at least some record of what that generation of masters and elders had to offer. At the time there was no financial provision or expertise to start a systematic collection. The only ones who seemed to have enough interest and money to work with oral traditions were foreign scholars. Though a Public Records Act was promulgated in 1969 imposing the deposit of copies of taped material by researchers, there was no one to enforce this law until the appointment of Mr Sidibeh who was also charged with supervision of foreign scholars. By this time several universities have taught their students that it is a gesture of scholarly courtesy to deposit such works with ones host country.

Between 1971-1972 Ms Winifred Galloway, a PhD scholar from Indiana University worked with Mr Sidibeh on a series of interviews on the political history of pre-colonial Gambia. This research essentially became a pilot study for the kind of work prepared for the cultural archives. In 1974, the Cultural Archives became the Oral History and Antiquities Division (OHAD), and was detached from the Records Office and moved to the site of the present National Museum. In 1975 Dr Galloway returned to OHAD under the auspices of the Peace Corps and between 1997 and 1980 other Peace Corps volunteers contributed in editing and organising publications.

By 1981 the staff was further augmented with the appointment of a Gambian Research Officer and an Antiquities Officer. The Research Officer was assigned the study of Jola traditions and the collection of their material culture for the museum, while the Antiquities Officer took on the job of management and preservation of monuments and heritage sites.

This in brief is the genesis of the oral archives and partially the history of the National Centre for Arts and Culture which is responsible for the archive, as well as museums and heritage sites, and the development of the creative and performing arts in the Gambia.

Today the Research and Documentation Division has a collection of over 5000 audio-visual recordings that are fundamental to understanding the history of the Gambia in particular, and the greater Senegambia in general. The material relates to inter-alia, the empire of Kaabu, a powerful federated kingdom that governed the regions of Gambia, southern Senegal (Casamance) and northern Guinea-Bissau from the late 13th to the mid 19th centuries. The areas covered include relations with neighbouring Fuuta Jalon in present-day Guinea-Conakry (18th-19th centuries); the origins of Kaabu in the 13th century, and the federation's subsequent social structure; the relationship between various ethnic groups in the region dating back at least to the 18th and 19th centuries. The recordings were made between the 1960s and 1980s, but as history in Africa is an oral genre, they relate strongly to pre-industrial societies in this part of Africa. These recordings covering Gambian, Senegalese and Bissau-Guinean history mean that the collection is one of the most extensive in the West African sub-region. The collection could serve as a research centre for the University of The Gambia. If better preserved and publicized, it would certainly attract a greater number of scholars to do research in The Gambia, and could help in revitalizing interest in pre-colonial Western African states in the global academy.

The importance of the collection is accentuated by its breadth. The fact that the material relates to the whole sub-region and not just The Gambia alone make the holdings of great historical value. Moreover, the importance of this region in early Atlantic history means that this importance transcends even the sub-region and relates to whole global historical process of the last several centuries. Adding to the importance of the collection is the sad loss of the oral history archive in Guinea-Bissau during the civil war there in 1998.

Research: The RDD is indeed the research arm of the NCAC. It supports the research component in all the other sectors of the NCAC such as in museum exhibition development, music, and literature and for administrative purposes. The RDD also used to have a Cultural Advisory Services which conducted research for NGOs and other institutions interested in data connected to culture to support development projects. Research remains an ongoing element in the RDD mandate. The output of the research done by RDD staff finds its way into the oral archives.

The RDD also issues research permits to external scholars interested in researching on culture, history, and traditions in The Gambia. At a fee, the scholar is issued a permit which enables him to access the RDD resources and historic and cultural sites throughout the country. The research permit could also facilitate immigration formalities for foreign scholars. One conditionality for the issuance of the permit is that the scholar must deposit a copy of their research findings at the RDD. In this way, the RDD collection of tapes and monographs continues to grow.

Library Services: The RDD has an extensive library of books and monographs on various topics covered by the NCAC mandate such as musicology, museology, archaeology, history, and traditions. There is also a newspapers library holding bound volumes of Gambian newspapers published in the past thirty years such as Senegambia Sun, Daily Observer, Point, Topic Magazine etc.

Most recently, a poetry library is being hosted at the RDD aimed at promoting the reading culture, especially among children.

Audio visual collections: The RDD has 5000 audio tapes on various aspects of Gambian history, culture, genealogy, traditions, folklore and music. These are in various media such as cassettes, reels, CDs and now a large part has been digitized. Most of these audio files have also been transcribed into English from the national language originals and the transcriptions are kept in files, which are also being digitized.

A small part of the tapes are videos of Gambian ceremonies and festivals.

The studio: There is now within the RDD a well-equipped studio where technicians work to transfer audio and video tapes from their original media into digital copies. The studio also has got the facilities to record and play back sound and video.

Monuments and Sites

Nearly every village or district in the country is endowed with significant monuments and cultural sites. Those monuments and sites whose significance transcends their local boundaries go through a process specified in the NCAC Act to be declared national monument. Further, those sites with outstanding universal significance are nominated for inscription in the UNESCO World Heritage List.

UNESCO World Heritage Sites

At present The Gambia has two inscriptions in the UNESCO World Heritage List. These are: 1. Kunta Kinteh Island (formerly James Island) and Related Sites, which was inscribed in the World Heritage List in 2003. The site is a serial inscription of several sites that form a historical continuum which illustrate outstanding universal value.

Kunta kinteh Island and Related Sites was inscribed under criteria iii and vi of the criteria for inscription stipulated in the World Heritage and consists of the following sites:

1. Kunta Kinteh Island, located 30 km away from the mouth of the River Gambia;

2. The ruins of the first Portuguese settlement at San Domingo, located on the north bank of the river close to James Island;

3. The ruins of the French and Portuguese settlements at Albreda and Juffureh which are located 1 km west of San Domingo (CFAO

Building, Maurel Freres Building and Portuguese Church);

4. The Mandingo village of Juffureh, which was popularized by Alex Haley's 'Roots', and the riverside settlement of Albreda;

5. Fort Bullen, located at Barra in the mouth of the river on the north bank.

6. The Six-gun battery, located in Banjul on the south bank of the mouth of the river opposite Fort Bullen.

According to the World Heritage Committee's citation, "these sites together present a testimony to the main periods and facets of the encounter between Africa and Europe along the River Gambia, a historical continuum stretching from pre-colonial and pre-slavery times to independence. The site is particularly significant for its relation to the beginning of the slave trade and its abolition and also documents early access to the interior of Africa".

The Stone Circles of the Senegambia, the second Gambian world heritage site was listed in 2006 under criteria I and iii. This is also a serial inscription and consists of four sites, two of which are found in Senegal (Sine Ngayene and Wanar), and the other two in The Gambia (Wassu and Kerbatch). The four large groups of stone circles represent an extraordinary concentration of over 1,000 monuments in a band 100 km wide along some 350 km of the River Gambia. The four groups cover 93 stone circles and numerous tumuli and burial mounds, some of which have been excavated to reveal material that suggest dates between 3rd century BC and 16th century AD. Together the stone circles of laterite pillars and their associated burial mounds present a vast sacred landscape created over more than 1,500 years, and reflect a prosperous, highly organized and lasting society1.

Sacred Sites

Sacred Pools

The three sacred crocodile pools of Katchikally in Bakau, Folongko in Kartong and Berending are primarily fertility shrines where, for generations, people have sought help for their problems. Bringing kola nuts as offerings, women come to cure their infertility, men to reverse bad fortune in business, parents to seek protection for their children during the trials of circumcision, wrestlers to achieve victory and more. As Ousman Bojang, the present custodian of Katchikally, squarely put it, *"The purpose of the pool is to bring peace to the people"*. If the correct procedures are followed it is believed certain that before a year passes the desires of the supplicant will be met.

The reptiles in these pools are Nile crocodiles which can grow up to 4.5 metres long and may live for over century. The pools at Bakau and kartong are fed by springs and are covered with a floating plant called water lettuce or 'pakungo', while the Berending pool is fed by salt water from nearby streams. A crocodile pool can be visited at the Abuko Nature Reserve though it is not thought to be a sacred place.

Katchikally

According to the legend handed down the Bojang family line, crocodiles were first brought to the pool on the instructions of Katchikally herself, the presiding spirit of the pool. Ousman Bojang, recounting how his family came to be the custodians of Katchikally recalls that his ancestor Ncooping Bojang and his family were the first people to settle in Bakau. One morning whilst sitting in their compound, "Nyamankala", a woman approached them in great hurry. *"Old man"*, she said to Ncooping, *"my child has fallen into a well, please help me get him out"*. Ncooping sent his two sons, Tambaasi and Jaali to help and they took the child out unharmed. It was then that the woman reveaed to them that nothing had actually happened to the child. She had come to find out whether they were troublemakers. But since they demonstrated their kindness by taking the child out of the well, she decided to reveal to them the importance of the place. *"God has blessed us with this well you see. He has given it the power to make child-bearing easy."* The two brothers and the woman returned to the compound and told the ageing man all that the woman had said, and why she had chosen them. "God has given this well to me, and I in turn give it to you people", she explained. The legend has it that Katchikally was the woman's name and she was a spirit dwelling in the bush who appeared to them in female form. Ousman adds that by saying and doing certain things Katchikally will appear again. His father taught him the means of doing this, but so far he has never tried it because he is too frightened.

The crocodiles at Katchikally live on a diet of frogs found in the vicinity and occasionally *bonga* fish brought by members of the Bojang family. The two crocodiles originally brought on the instructions of Katchikally have now multiplied to over forty. At the height of the rainy season when the pool is at its fullest young crocodiles are often washed out of the pool.

When a person comes to seek a blessing at the pool, he or she comes with kola nuts which are shared amongst the members of the Bojang Kunda (family), and prayers are said to fulfil his or her wishes. An elder of the family brings water from the pool, the water is blessed, and the person is ritually washed. The ceremony is completed with drumming and dancing. Before leaving, the person is asked to abstain from unbecoming behaviour, for example a woman should abstain from adultery. When the person's wish is fulfilled, they must come back to make it known.

Kartong Folongko: The custodians of the Folongko pool in Kartong are the Jaiteh family. The presiding spirit of the pool is said to be the daughter of Katchikallly, and so the two pools are closely interconnected.

Berending: The Berending pool serves the same purpose as Katchikally and Folongko though it is fed by salt water and does not have 'pakungo' on its surface. It is nevertheless a sacred place.

Sacred Groves, Trees and Stone Altars: Sacred groves, trees and stone altars constitute another category of cultural sites which exist throughout The Gambia. Like other cultural sites they are said to have the potential to ward off evil and bring good to individuals and the community. Various people, particularly the Jola, have sacred groves where they perform religious and other ceremonies such as initiation. Usually a sanctuary for animal and bird life, because of their lush vegetation, such groves are said to be under the charge of or occupied by spirits or divinities. Jola divinities are known to be most effective for disclosing the identities of thieves. Trees usually found in such groves include the baobab and a variety of fruit trees which are often forbidden for eating. It is forbidden to collect firewood from sacred groves.

Mythical' trees can be found in a number of villages around the country. They are considered sacred by many people who make offerings and sacrifices and say prayers around or under them. They too are associated with God and other spiritual beings. Sometimes they serve as landmarks or mark the graves of legendary people in the society. Stones, hills and caves are also venerated. They too are associated with spirits and divinities and people consult them for their welfare, bringing along offerings of money and food which they deposit in the vicinity.

Sannementereng: The Saano Kunda family of Brufut, are the traditional custodians of Sannementereng. They hold the site in trust for the people of Busumbala who hosted them when they first arrived from Kaabu in the east. The legend has it that one of the elders of Saano kunda was a hunter and in his hunting exploits came across an old man from Busumbala praying in a clearing in the bush that presently constitutes Sannementereng. The old man insisted that he join him in prayers and afterwards revealed that the site is a sacred place and anything prayed for at the spot will be achieved. Hunting was also forbidden within the grounds. When the people of Saano Kunda decided to settle with their host they asked for a piece of land, which they preferred to be near the sea. The host consented to allocate them the area around Sannementereng on condition that they would take care of the place and serve as guides to whoever came for prayers at the site. Proceeds realised from offerings at the site should be shared between Saano Kunda and Busumbala. The ancestor of Saano Kunda agreed to the terms and named their settlement "Tento" (presently Brufut), a Mandinka term for temporary shelter. Soon people started flocking to the site for prayers from all over West Africa because *"whatever they pray for, they see"* Some come to keep vigil for a week, others for a month. During this time they are provided with food by the Saano Kunda family. In return they pay a fee which also covers the use of the hut that was built for those keeping vigil.

When people come for prayers they report to Saano Kunda from where someone takes them to the site and bathes them in a well at the bottom of the cliff, before they start their prayers. People come to pray for solutions to all sorts of problems, unmarried women to get husbands, barren women to get children, etc. Many return to express their satisfaction and give presents to the custodians.

Saanementereng has been in existence for over 300 years. Its guardian spirit, it is said, is a Muslim and consequently does not do anything bad.

Farankunko: This is a sacred grove located on the outskirts of Dumbutu in the Lower River Region. The land belongs to the Colley Kunda kabilo (family clan) and kafoo (social groups) are found in the area. The grove is used by the whole village to perform special ceremonies usually organised by women. Offerings of kola nut, food, money and clothes are made at the site. The ceremonies are normally accompanied by singing, dancing, cooking and eating. The site is mostly used for praying for rain after long periods of drought.

Santangba: Santangba is the site of a sacred tree located on the outskirts of Brikama, the administrative capital of the Western Coast Region. It is said that when the people of Brikama were leaving

Mali it was predicted that there was a special spot where they should settle. They arrived at Kokotali which the king's marabout identified was the place predicted to them. They cleared the area around a 'Santango' tree and settled. From that spot they later moved to Brikama. The site of the tree was therefore regarded as sacred because it was their first settlement. Today, before children are taken for circumcision they must offer prayers at the site. The original tree has now been replaced by a *'nya yiro'* fruit tree. It is believed that wherever a 'santango' tree is found it marks the route taken by their ancestors when they migrated from Mali.

To get there ask for the Chief's compound in Brikama. From there you can be provided a guide to take you to the site.

Berewuleng:
This site is a grove the centrepiece of which is a huge boulder stone. Overlooking the beach at Sanyang village in the Western Division, legend has it that the place was the site of a mosque used by a Muslim jinn who had a long beard and was often seen going to the spot with prayer beads in his hand. Because people believe that the site was his mosque, they go there to say prayer and take along money and food which they place on the boulder. Visitors must

however be accompanied by an elder from the village.

To get there ask for the Alkalo's compound in Sanyang where you can be provided with a guide to take you to the site.

Tombs and Burial Sites

Monuments to the dead constitute another category of Cultural Sites in The Gambia. These usually house the corpses of famous religious leaders, chiefs or soldiers. In most cases the maintenance of such monuments is a family responsibility. Those wishing to visit the sites do not need to consult with the families to do so, unless special prayers are needed. It is not unusual to find devotees of the people buried in such tombs also taking care of the site.

Sait Matty's Tomb

A rectangular block structure about two metres in height standing in the front garden of the Sun Beach Hotel at Cape Point in Bakau marks the burial site of Sait Matty Ba, a Muslim Fula who led campaigns in the civil war between the Soninkes and Marabouts during the late 1880s. Sait Matty was the son of Maba Diakhou Ba, a devout scholar and jidhadist born of Denianke origins in the Futa Toro. At the height of his jihad Maba moved through the Senegambia displacing the Wollof and Serer populations, ravaging Jola land, destroying the Mandinka kingdoms and posing a threat to French and British interests in the area. Maba was killed 1867 and was succeeded by his brother Momodou Ndare who faced much opposition to his rule. He was challenged by one of his lieutenants, Biran Ceesay, who started another civil war in 1877 in Baddibu and Sine-Saloum which disrupted trade and agriculture on the North Bank. Then in 1884 Sait Matty began fighting Ndare for control of his father's forces and railed against Biran Ceesay for his inheritance of the rulership of Baddibu. Three years later a peace treaty was negotiated with collaboration of the French and British whereby Sait Matty was to recognise Biran Ceesay's Lordship over the towns in Sine-Saloum and Niumi and Ceesay was to acknowledge Sait Matty's over-Lordshhip throughout the entire area.

However, Sait Matty soon invaded Sine-Saloum. The French warned him to withdraw, he refused, and with the co-operation of the king of Sine-Saloum, the French pursued him. Sait Matty fled to The Gambia, took refuge at Albreda, and on 11th May 1887 surrendered to the British.

His defeat plunged Baddibu into a new civil war which threatened to spill over into Sine-Saloum. The French therefore decided to take control of Sait Matty's towns, disposed of two of Biran Ceesay's chiefs and authorised local chiefs to collect tributes in Baddibu. Sait Matty then moved to Bakau where he lived quietly until his death in 1897.

Musa Molloh's Tomb

A Muslim Fula, Musa Molloh Balde was the second ruler of the Empire of Fuladu and son of Alfa Molloh, the founder of the kingdom and a great hunter and king. Fuladu was part of the Fula Confederation that stretched from the Gambia River to the Corubal River in Guinea Bissau and incorporated both British and French territory.

Raiders were annually sent to invade the Upper River Area because the region was under the control of exiled Marabouts who were previously part of the confederation. Shortly after Musa Molloh was born, Alfa Molloh began his uprising (1867-68) against animist Mandinka neighbours who were persecuting the Fula population. Part of his military efforts included establishing Islam wherever he gained control. Alfa Molloh died in 1874 and was succeeded by his brother, Bakary Demba, who was to bequeath the throne to Musa Molloh. Disputes arose over the inheritance but Musa Molloh decided to recognise his uncle as overlord, although for the next decade there were conflicts between the two. Aware of the dangers of civil war, Musa Molloh went south of the Casamance. After Bakary Demba's death in 1884,

Musa Molloh became sole ruler of Fuladu. He became a very useful ally for the British, French and local West African Government in The Gambia as he acted as mediator between these various groups when trying to settle ethnic differences. In 1887 he assisted the French against Momodou Lamin Drammeh, a Soninke marabout who rebelled against foreign domination. In the 1890's Musa Molloh co-operated with the British in fighting against Foday Kabba, an extremely powerful marabout war leader based in the Kombos who was one of the last opponents of colonial rule. By 1892 Musa Molloh proclaimed himself supreme ruler throughout all of British and French Fuladu. His territory lay on both sides of the arbitrary colonial boundaries, but he lived on the French side. In 1901 he handed over control of British Fuladu to the Government of The Gambia. This transfer made possible the British administration of the protectorate system for all of The Gambia except St. Mary's Island.

An ordinance of 1902 incorporated Fuladu into the colony which halted the slave trade that Musa Molloh was still engaged in. Two years later, feeling pressured by French colonial interests and being accused by them of tyrannical conduct, Musa Molloh retreated to British territory and settled in Kesser Kunda near Georgetown. Not appreciating his autocratic manner and urged on by the allegations of his enemies, the British exiled Musa Molloh to Sierra Leone in 1919. He was allowed to return to The Gambia in 1923 but without any political power. He died at Kesser Kunda in 1931. His son Cherno Balde was the final ruler of the Empire of Fuladu.

Musa Molloh is renowned as a famous warrior and leader of troops as well as being a skilful diplomat in being able to deal successfully with both the French and British in the midst of Senegambian politics. His tomb was restored in 1971 and was declared a National Monument in 1974. The present structure was built in 1987 in collaboration with the Senegalese Government.

Other Cultural Sites
These include: sacred wells; sites used by renowned personalities for prayers; ant hills; cemeteries; stone circles or isolated stone pillars; caves; mosques; etc. At times associated with special powers, some of them are venerated by individuals and communities and used for prayers and offerings.

Sand Dune Mosque
Kenye-kenye Jamango is a Mandinka term which literally translates as Sand Dune Mosque. This referred to a makeshift mosque located on the sand dunes overlooking Gunjur beach about 1km from the

fishing centre, which is currently under development. The mosque, associated grounds, buildings and rocks are all regarded as sacred because the site provided sojourn for the Kalifat'ul Tijanniyya Sheikh Umar Taal (Leader of the Tijaaniyya Sect in West Africa) during his Islamisation mission in West Africa.

The importance of Sheikh Umar (1793-1864) in the propagation of Islam in the West African sub-region is well documented by his disciples, historians and writers. He is renowned as the man who most significantly earned himself the title Khalifat'ul Tijanniyya through his teachings and holy wars. His pilgrimage to Mecca (1828-1831) and other centres of Islam in the Middle East helped a great deal in accelerating his mission. During his return trip from Mecca he went through Cairo, Bornu, Sokoto, and Madina before reaching Futa Jallon towards the end of 1840. Throughout his journey news of his greatness and erudition preceded him. He was able to eclipse prestigious Marabouts particularly of the Qadiriyya sect which until then was the dominant brotherhood in West Africa.

As one of the notable leaders of the Tijanniyya, with authority from Muhamad Al Ghali, Sheikh Umar took it upon himself to fight 'paganism' and challenge the political and social order of the old Muslim theocracies and replace them with a new branch of militant Islam. In 1852 he embarked on a series of military campaigns, imposing his authority from the Senegambia to the Niger. He attracted disciples from all over West Africa including the Aku, or freed slaves of African origin, in Sierra Leone. His Senegambian tour to the north got him into conflict with the Jahanke Marabouts and Qadiriyya sympathisers who did not believe in Jihads as a means of converting people to Islam. He was more successful in the rest of Senegambia where prominent personalities like Alfa Molo and Maba Jahu Bah adopted the Tijanniyya Tarikh in addition to thousands of Mandinka, Wollof, Fula, Soninke and Kasonke disciples who later joined him. Sheikh Umar met up with the French on two occasions, always assuring them of his intention to establish Islam. His vision of establishing a vast Islamic entity posed a threat not only to the established secular order but to the new territorial ambitions of European powers who had started arriving on the Senegambia Coastline.

According to oral sources Sheikh Umar came to The Gambia during the later part of his life when he had adopted peaceful Islamisation as a means of increasing his following. He came to Banjul via Barra in the North Bank Region, and on arrival spent a day under a big fig tree at the Albert Market in Banjul. From there he was taken to Dobson Street by one

Ebrima Faye's wife, whose new-born son he demanded should be named after him. As predicted the boy Sheikh Umar Faye, grew up to be a great scholar, holding positions of trust in both government and the private sector and making valiant contributions during the Second World War. Sheikh Umar Taal also sojourned at Cape Point behind the present site of the Sun Beach Hotel. Here he prayed for peace and protection for the people ad since then the site became sacred and is still visited by people who hold him in high regard. Most importantly, he visited Gunjur, a village on the coast. He found the place serene and suited to holy worship and as a result spent more time at this site than anywhere else in The Gambia. Here, under the shade of trees and huge boulder stones, he prayed at seven spots for God's guidance and favour. This is how the sacred ground at Gunjur became famous, attracting Islamic scholars and pilgrims from all over West Africa. On his departure the old mosque was built to cater for visitors, some of whom stay several nights in makeshift huts to conduct their vigils.

Touba Kolong

During Maba's attacks on the Soninke in Sine-Saloum many refugees fled to Niumi particularly around Barra. But due to Amer Faal creating disturbances up-river the British moved about 2000 of the refugees to Bantang Kiling near Albreda and placed them under the leadership of the animist Wollof ruler Masamba Korki.

Masamba Korki and his people suffered periodic harassment from the Muslim Nuiminka, and in 1866 Faal's followers stole some of their cattle. A Colonel D'Arcy thus organised a punitive expedition of Europeans and Niuminkas to the village of Touba Kolong where Faal had his headquarters. Touba Kolong was protected by a triple log stockade. Led by D'Arcy, 17 volunteers, including 15 men of the Fourth West Indian Regiment, advanced to make a breach in the first stockade. Only two men, Samuel Hodges and Boswell, managed to reach it. Working with axes under heavy gunfire they made a hole in the wall but Boswell was killed in the attempt. D'Arcy was first through the hole followed by Hodges who immediately began to hack through the other two stockades. The rest of the troops entered the village and with the aid of bayonets took control, though the Muslims fought hard and suffered 300 casualties before yielding. Hodges was later awarded a Victoria Cross for his bravery being one of the first Africans to receive this medal of honour from the British.

Oral sources provide a different account of the battle. According to these accounts, beyond the stockades the villagers had dug a well and covered it with leaves and sticks such that when the attackers penetrated the stockade they fell into the well leading to a massive loss of life on the part of the Europeans. To this day Touba Kolong is popular more for this historical ruse than for anything else. The site of the well, which is marked by a huge depression, has been fenced in by the villagers and is now turning into a tourist attraction. Touba Kolong is on the North Bank road leading to Albreda.

Literature (and Publishing)

Background:

Literature writing and publishing industry in the country is vibrant and growing. Until the 1960s, there was not much Gambian literary writing in English due to the poor educational attainment during colonial period. However, from the mid-1960s, Lenrie Peters (1932-2009) a UK trained surgeon published his first novel The Second Round (Heinemann, 1965) and this book is seen as the flame which ignited modern Gambian literature in English. Peters was in the same generation as Soyinka, Achebe and Okigbo. His themes were mainly on colonial rule and the foibles and failures of the immediate post-independence African regimes.

Mrs Hannah Jawara aka Ramatulie Kinteh, wrote several well acclaimed plays in the early 1960s while she was First Lady, the consort of Sir Dawda Kairaba Jawara, Gambia's first President. She was one of Black Africa's first published women writers. Gabriel Roberts' plays were broadcast, performed by the BBC African Service in 1970, and later published in the prestigious African Writers' series. In the 1970s, a new wave of literary writings emerged in Bathurst (the old name for Banjul) the Gambian capital in the form of literary magazine called "Ndaanan", Wollof word for Champion.

When Ndaanan closed in 1976, there was another long furlough in Gambian literary writings till the 1980s when a new corps of writers such as Swaebou Conateh, Nana Grey Johnson and Tijaan Sallah emerged to animate the literary milieu in the country. These writers although highly determined and talented had to confront the fact of lack of local publishing houses and poor distribution (there was only one bookshop in the country) and low literacy. Albeit, other Gambians in the diaspora like Ebou Dibba published (Chaff on the Wind and Fafa) and Baba Sillah a blind man also published (When the Monkey Talks).

The emergence of the first regular daily newspaper in Banjul in 1992, the Daily Observer, generated another generation of writers who now published prose, poetry and essays in the pages of the daily newspaper. Sheriff Bojang, Baba Galleh Jallow, Mariama Khan, Hassoum Ceesay, Ebou Gaye could be counted among this Daily Observer generation. Most of them have gone onto become accomplished writers and authors since the early 2000s.

Publishing Industry:

For a long time, there was no professional book publishing outfit outside the government owned Printing Department. In the early 2000s, Fulladu Publishers established shop as the first professional publisher in the country taking on many new and established writers in literature, history, school textbook etc. Since then new publishing companies have emerged like Sukai Mbye Bojang of Educational Services, Baobab Printers etc. and self-publishers like Patience Sonko Godwin, Hamadi Secka, Momodou Sabally etc... Gambians continue to write their life experiences in prose, poetry and play; also, aspects of our history, culture and geography are being written and published by Gambians. However, the publishing industry remains largely untapped due to financial and capacity challenges such that authors have to handle the marketing of the published works. The Gambia's rich oral literature in the form of stories, proverbs, fables etc. is still largely untapped and remains a huge reservoir of the collective memory of the people.

The National Centre for Arts and Culture Act, Copyright Act and Gambia Library Act all require publishers and printers to submit copies of works as deposits. The Copyright Act of 2004 will assist in the strengthening of the book publishing industry as it secures firmly the intellectual rights of writers and publishers. Besides providing this vital legal framework for writers and publishers, the government's Ministry of Basic Education also promotes the reading of books by Gambian authors in schools. In order to make Gambians continue to chronicle their experiences in literature, a robust book publishing industry would be nurtured. Also, reading culture would be revived by promotion of Gambian literature and writings in our schools and colleges to give exposure to local talent, and the building of Regional and Town libraries. A literary award would be established to reward leading Gambian writers and authors.

The literary fraternity has been measuring tremendous successes within the past 3 years through The Writers Association; authors have published and launched several books with a significant rise in female and young writers. A day for the writers is being culled aside as part of a calendar of events for the years, where books can be reviewed with recitations of poetry and so on. The objective is to rejuvenate the reading culture of Gambians, showcase their work and enhance our literary cadres.

To achieve these objectives our main strategic partner is the Writers' Association of the Gambia (WAG) which was established in 2009 with the following objectives:

a) Promote, encourage and facilitate creative and other technical writing in The Gambia;

b) Promote links among Gambian writers to enhance their collective and individual literary capacities, productivity and interests, nationally and internationally;

c) Promote the writing of technical, research and school books and materials for the Gambia;

d) Co-ordinate the publication and dissemination of literary texts by Gambians;

e) Establish high standards in the writing, production and publication of texts from Gambian writers residing in The Gambia;

f) Foster and enhance the patriotic and constructive role of Gambian and other resident writers in national development;

g) Ensure the protection by law of the works and originality of Gambian writers, in particular, and of other writers in The Gambia, in general;

h) Promote and protect the intellectual property rights of writers and monitor the stringent application of Copyright Laws of the Gambia;

i) Facilitate documentation and preservation of all published materials by Gambian writers and when possible archiving them.

j) Present the Dr. **Lenrie Peters Memorial Lecture & Award** annually to a deserving author and other incentives to writers.

k) To do all things that help to promote the aims and objectives of the association.

Music

Background:
Gambian music started flourishing from the early 1960s after independence with the rise of the

maestro bands of the Super Eagles, Guelewar and later Ifang Bondi until the 80s. From the 1980s till 2000 the music scene suffered because of the departure of the earlier generation of musicians to seek greener pastures abroad and the rise of the Senegalese Mbalax music. Congolese and later Nigerian music also gained momentum with the rise of FM radio broadcasts. However, since the mid-2000, there has been a noticeable revival of Gambian music through rap and Afro- Manding. The renaissance of the traditional Manding kora music has taken a new dimension with its introduction of live bands instead of the single kora player as a griot.

The current music scene is characterized by 3 classes comprising the Traditional music, Contemporary rappers and live bands playing different genres of music. The Traditional musicians category consist of the local griots, traditional communicators, local ensembles, etc. whilst the contemporary genres consist of the rappers of Mbalax / Afro- Manding, Hip- Hop/ RnB, and Reggae / Dancehall. Of recent, most of these groups have transformed into the live bands category. These evolutions are mainly propelled by nationalist demands to patronize our own music and the economic sense of reducing the influx of foreign artistes' performances in the Gambia.

Jaliba Kuyateh spear headed the genre of turning the Kora into a live band. This evolution prompted the movement of so many contemporary rappers from play- back musicians to live instrument players. They eventually form bands or work with a commissioned backing-band such as Humanity Starz and Holy Family Bands. Today, the likes of Jali Madi Kanuteh, Mandingmorry and Bai Babu are signed by budding record labels such as Joluv Arts, Musico, etc… who also take up the task of marketing their artists abroad. Gee, Jalex, Benjamin, Killa Ace, Badibunka, ST, TSmallz, Balla Ranks etc… are currently making waves and are storming the home stage with increasingly larger crowds. There are other Gambian musicians abroad who are also doing well and come home once a while for concerts with their band members. Prominent amongst them are Sing-a–teh (Freaky Joe), Rebellion-The Recaller, Mohawk, Egalitarian and Sona Jobarteh.

Music Industry:

The Gambian music industry has under gone a significant strive since 2012 and 2013 with 14 and 12 respective new album launchings and numerous crowd pulling performances from 11 promising artists on live instrument bands. This is further boosted with numerous international performances in the UK, USA, Europe and Venezuela. Home spectacles also have gone up with the Gambian music showbiz hosted periodically at Alliance, Joko Brikama, Jama Hall and now the Open Mic Festival at the Independence Stadium, which is a privately supported musical bonanza and showcases our young talents in December for the 7th year consecutively; during this event new talents are discovered and ready to be nurtured. Therefore, the music industry is shaping up with talented crowd pulling singers, technical composers /arrangers / publishers, producers, promoters, live band instrumentalists and record labels, which are some of the structures needed to set up an industry.

The Gambian music scene fanfares more locally and its market potential internationally is quite huge amongst the Gambians in the diaspora and European music festivals; meaning Gambian musicians are mostly either invited by Gambian resident associations abroad on certain events or by European music festivals occasionally. Instead most of the musicians play at nightclubs, restaurants or bars and rarely on their own concerts excepting Jaliba Kuyateh who manages to perform in large auditoriums. Albeit, The distribution of their music products especially CDs and music videos are impeded by piracy amongst the Gambian community, a pirate will buy only one product and duplicate into several volumes for sale to the Gambians abroad in the absence of bilateral copyright protection between the Gambia and that country.

For over a century, the Gambia did not have a relevant and responsive copyright law to protect the creativity of its citizens. This has contributed to blunt the creative edge of artists in the country. The promulgation of the Gambia Copyright Act 2004 has therefore filled in major lacunae in our cultural milieu. The Gambia Copyright Act, 2004 assures full moral and economic rights to works which fall 'under literary, artistic, musical, sound recordings, audio-visual work; choreographic work, derivative and programme carrying signal. The Act also protects folklore against reproduction or public performance for commercial purposes. It gives economic rights to authors and creators and protects translated works. The Act therefore has gone a long way in the promotion of intellectual, moral and economic rights of Gambian creators.

The Copyright Act also provides for the setting up of a Collecting Society of the Gambia (CSG) charged with the collection and distribution of royalties and also safeguards their interests abroad.

The department meets its mandate through working with the Gambia Music Union (MUSIGAM)
MUSIGAM Constitution

Gambia Music Union (Musicians):
The Gambia Music Union's mission is;

To develop a cultural music industry and creative cadres centered on the understanding of and the appreciation of Gambian Music and the music of all Gambian ethnic groups.

Their sole aim is:

a) To co-ordinate music events and festivals in collaboration with National Centre for Arts and Culture.

b) To promote the appreciation of Gambian music and culture nationally and internationally.

c) To create a better understanding of our multi ethnic Gambian traditional music

d) To promote and create National and International development and education projects, for association members.

e) To promote education on music industry and practice.

f) To create branches of the union in community centres throughout Gambia.

g) To eradicate music piracy in Gambia in the interest of all musicians.

h) To foster and support close relationships with International Musicians Association, and participate in Pan African Music initiatives.

i) To protect the interests of musicians employed within Gambia.

j) To collaborate with international organisations in the promotion of Gambian music, musicians and cultural groups.

k) Protect members against misuse of their works by broadcasting, performance or illegal recording.

l) Collaborate in the formation of Copyright and Royalty Collection Agency and devise protective measure to ensure against piracy.

Theatre (Drama & Dance)

Like all other nations, the Gambia is endowed with skillful and talented youths engaged in the performing arts, either out of passion, or for gainful employment. They all aspire towards greater success and recognition so as to be able to make a living out of the industry. Theatre, drama and dance are growing by leaps and bounds in The Gambia. Recently, this form of arts has become a popular form of cultural and artistic expression and it affords youth, women groups in particular, a strong forum for the exercise of cultural right and expression. Story telling based on ancient Gambian lores and tales, riddles and local games are also enriching aspects of Gambian oral performances.

The rise in the popularity of drama could be ascribed to the advent of a national TV service and the growth in FM stations which can expose these groups to a bigger audience. In the absence of a formal school of performing arts where they can undergo structured learning on the tools of the trade, most of their productions tended to be mediocre. There is only one purpose built theatre facility called Ebunjan Theatre. Earlier the Alliance Francaise amphitheatre provided the only facility for the staging of performances. More stage shows are now taking place, with improvised casts at the Ebunjan Theatre, whilst associations like the Gambia Youth Actors Association (GAMYAA) and the Comedian Association of the Gambia (CAG) continue to frequent the stage at Alliance Francaise. A number of drama groups such as Gopp Garr, Fansung Jamanoo, Bolondala, etc... have also progressed into producing films in DVDs and drama pieces for the television

Fashion and Beauty Pageant

Background:

In The Gambia the first recorded Beauty Pageant was organized by Roxy Vous at the UAC Tennis Lawn in 1963, when the glamorous Miss Joana Jahumpa won what was then "Miss Bathurst". In 1965, as part of The Gambia's Independence celebrations, government included a Miss Independence Beauty Contest in the program following a suggestion by the METTA Youth Club. The Miss Independence was well organized at the Independence gala and was one of the highlights of the celebrations. The competition was won by Miss Elizabeth Thomas now Mrs. Elizabeth Renner, Ex Speaker of the House of Representatives.

Motivated by the success of the Miss Independence pageant, the late Mr Val Phatty, the then director of Social Welfare Department, invited the Metta Youth Club to organise a contest to select a beauty queen who would represent The Gambia at a contest in the Middle East. That contest was the first Miss Gambia in the country and it was won by Ndey Jagne. She was the first beauty queen to represent The Gambia at the Miss World Pageant in 1965.Oumie Barry (1966), Janie Jack (1967), Mary Carayol (1968), and Princess Margaret Davies (1970).

After a lull of about a decade, in 1981 Atta Promotion started organizing pageants again. In 1983 Abi Janneh won the coveted crown. Abi Janneh proceeded to compete in the Miss World pageant where she won Miss Congeniality in that year. In1984, Mirabell Carayol won the Miss Gambia crown and also competed in Miss World. Baturu Jallow was Miss Gambia in 1985and competed in the Miss Universe contest. Baturu was later disqualified and replaced by Adam Sanneh who participated in the Miss World that year. The other winners were Rose Eunson in 1986; Ellen Forster in1987, Oumou Haidara Faye in 1988, Fatou Jarra in 1989. According to Mr George Gomez, Fatou Jarra (Mrs Houma) resigned for family reasons and the first runner-up, Ade Clarke was appointed to continue her reign. In 1990, Mai Coker was crowned Miss Gambia. Atta Promotions also organized a Miss Senegambia Contest in 1986.

In 1984, BanZig International established the Miss Senegambia Pageant on a formal basis and in1985 organized the first Miss Senegambia Beauty Contest with six contestants from Senegal and six contestants from The Gambia. To help select the contestants from The Gambia, the Banjul Branch of BanZig International organized the first Miss Gambia, BanZig. The winner of that coveted crown, Osai Gillen and the next five ladies in the competition represented The Gambia at Miss Senegambia1985 with Miss Gillen becoming the first runner-up. In1987, Monica Musa was crowned Miss Gambia (BanZig); in 1988, Jorjo Touray won the crown and in 1989 Majula Jallow was the winner. BanZig International organized the first Miss Senegambia at the Atlantic Hotel in 1985 and it was won by Santal Lobillo of Senegal.

In 1987, the contest was held at the Teranga Hotel in Dakar under the chief patronage of the Mayor of Dakar and it was won by Monica Musa of The Gambia. The then president of Senegal, Mr. Abdou Diouf received the officials of BanZig International and Miss Monica Musa in audience at the presidential palace in Dakar and invited Miss Monica Musa as a special guest at the Senegal Independence anniversary dinner at state house that year.

In 1988, the competition was again held at the Atlantic Hotel in The Gambia and was won by Jorjo Touray of The Gambia. In 1989, the contest was held in Ziguinchor, Casamance and was won by Rohey

Gaye, commonly called "Gaiya" by her friends, from The Gambia.

The 1989 contest was the last time BanZig International organized Miss Senegambia due to the dissolution of the Senegambia Confederation. As a result of this and also the absence of Miss Gambia for almost five years, Gomis Promotion was registered and took over the organisation of not only Miss Gambia but Miss Tourism, Miss Elegance and Miss Jongama and on two occasions organized Miss Roots.

Fashion Design

For a long time, The Gambia was seen as a minor in the fashion world. Today the fashion industry in the country has really come of age, as The Gambia can now boast of having numerous internationally acclaimed designers who are mostly self taught. A passion for real African garments has led many well-known and top-rated designers to join the industry and today they are making waves in the fashion scene. One of the earliest to become a house hold name was the late Musukebba Drammeh, who capitalized on the tourism industry with her specialty in tie and dye and batik. Nowadays many young and middle- aged women and men have established workshops housing tailors who produce their designs whilst they use the same outlets as showrooms. They produce designs mixing fabrics and using embroidery with admirable results and styles that are a mixture of both vintage and modern.

As The Gambia gets an even younger and more exposed population, the desire to explore creativity and re-create the tourist industry has brought in a flurry of ideas such as Fashion Weekend Gambia, Gambia Fashion Night, Gambia Next Top Model, Queen of Companies etc... attracting countless young and talented designers who explore an infusion of Gambian and African roots. In 2010, the Association of Fashion Designers Gambia (AFDG) was formed and now not only working to promote fashion design but also support causes for the empowerment of women.

The Department for the Performing Arts collaborates with The Association of Fashion Designers Gambia on matters of fashion and beauty pageantry.

Film

The Gambia is not very renowned in the film production world. The country is more of a consumer than a producer of films. There have not been popular productions from The Gambia in the genre of feature films or great documentaries with professional 35mm cameras. In fact the film that has done most in popularizing the Gambia was by Alex Harley "ROOTS" (1977), which was shot with 35mm camera and even partially shot in the Gambia with a wholly non-Gambian cast and crew.

Earlier in the late 1960s government had established the film unit under the Ministry of Information charged with documentation of audio visual images of state events and development issues. (refer to write up on film unit)

A few exceptions are the film 'Lamin' (1987) shot by Norwegian TV Broadcasting Corporation (NRK) with BETACAMS and using Gambian actors such as Sheikh Omar Jallow. The film maintained the top 10 slots for 10 weeks in Scandinavia. 'Aarow' (2006) by Amadou Sillah of Vinasha Productions shot in new digital format and has won an AMA award in 2006. There are a few that have also won other nominations recently including "The Hand of Fate" (2013) by Director Ibrahim Ceesay at the NAFCA Award in Washington and who's second film "Sarata" (2014) is currently being screened. Also a television series in HD format dubbed "Nakala" (2015) by Modou Lamin Touray – Sisquo is recently launched and is being broadcast on the Senegalese TV. . Most of those who now dabble in the industry obtained their training on-the-job as employees of private media houses or the one and only Gambia Radio and Television Services (GRTS).

In recent times the country is getting increasingly popular as a location for shooting films by producers of the sub-region, especially Nigerians. But most of the films shot in the country are realized by non-Gambian producers and directors, using largely Gambian casts and already popular actors/actresses from Nigeria to leverage the films in the international market. This situation in our perception is motivated by the relatively cheap cost of producing films in the country vis- a -vis the cost of services such as hotels. Other reasons include the growing appetite for youth to participate in films, either for artistic or economic reasons and the chance for one's talent to be spotted and given a break in the international arena. This compels them to look for opportunities to participate in films at any cost, at times paying for auditioning. At present there is no institute devoted to training film-makers.

At present the industry is characterized by productions directed at national television, be they commercials, documentaries or drama sketches, the latter mostly intended for sensitization on social or educational issues. In this scenario Government, NGOs, and commercial enterprises such as GSM service providers are the main sponsors/funding agents. The other category that is also gaining in momentum is that of those engaged in producing video clips for musicians. In the last 3 years the country has been witnessing more films by Gambians despite scarce funding especially for the making of feature films. Gambian productions are now featuring at film festivals such as Clap Ivoire in Abidjan, Durban Film Festival in South Africa, AMA Award of Nigeria.

It is not certain how much Gambian and non-Gambian producers realize from film consumption in the country in the absence of a functional Collective Management Society. What is certain is that most of the films in circulation are pirated. It is also obvious that piracy is the bane of the industry in The Gambia as well as the sub-region.

In 2004 a new copyright law was enacted replacing the colonial inheritance of 1912 which only covered printed material. At present the country has a Copyright Bureau under the NCAC and an independent Collecting Society both of which are struggling for resources to be fully functional.

Travel to and within Gambia

Travel to Banjul

Introduction:

Banjul, officially the City of Banjul (former name Bathurst until 1973), is the capital of the Republic of The Gambia, in West Africa, as well as the administrative centre of the country and the seat of government. The port city has a population of about 31,000 and is divided into 3 districts. Its land area is 12 sq km (4.6 sq. mi), and it is located on Saint Mary's Island, at the southern part of the Gambia River ria estuary. The flat island was leased by the British colonial government, from the King of Kombo, for 103 iron bars per annum in 1816, and the Bathurst settlement was named after the Secretary of State for the British Colonies, Lord Henry Bathurst.

Arrival

The Banjul capital is not usually the first stop for most visitors on flights to The Gambia; after landing at Yundum Airport, most tourists go straight to the beach resort hotels along the Atlantic coast, which are mostly in Bijilo, Brufut, Kololi, Kotu and Kerr Sering. There is however the beach based, 4 star, Atlantic Hotel.

There are three routes into the capital. If you are travelling by road from southern Gambia, the coastal resorts or from the airport past Serrekunda, you take the Banjul-Serrekunda Highway, driving past thick banks of mangroves in the Tanbi Wetland Complex to your right, on the way to Oyster Creek, which separates the mainland from the island, and is traversed by Denton Bridge. After the bridge, the road traces the west coastline of St. Mary's Island, until forking at Independence Drive, with Arch 22 in front of you, Wallace Cole Road to your right, Marina Parade to your left. The second route is to detour just before the city by turning right into Bund Road, this takes you to the ports area. The third route is from the north bank of the Gambia River or northern Senegal, through the Amdalai / Karang border crossing; you go by road to the ferry terminal at Barra (Niumi District) on the north bank of the Gambia River, from which a scheduled ferry service takes you across the river to the terminal on

Liberation Avenue in city's southern commercial district. Outside the terminal turn right to go towards the Royal Albert Market and the Atlantic Hotel; turn left and follow the Kankujereh Road north west to connect with the highway heading back towards Serrekunda.

Accommodation:

Swimming PoolDespite its distinctive appearance, The Gambia's capital city can't be thought of as everyone's idea of the idyllic holiday resort. Banjul has only one tourist-class hotel, the Atlantic Hotel. There are also a batch of 1 or 2 star hotels and guest houses in the centre of town, serving mostly travelling Africans. The best of these are a little tatty, while the worst often charge an hourly rate. However, even some of these are worth checking out for a budget-priced experience.

The Town:

Banjul's commercial centre is around the docks at the city's east end. Despite the port's small size it is a critical entryway for imports as well as exports, and the roads near the waterfront are often jammed with trucks and lorries waiting to load newly arrived consignments such as sugar, rice and cooking oil as they are offloaded from container ships. Some merchandise are destined for stores on Liberation and Ecowas Avenue as well as the Royal Albert

Market, others get transported inland and to other countries in West Africa via entrepot.

The area just inland from the port is Banjul's main shopping sector. You won't find shopping malls, large supermarkets or even shops with glass window displays as the business of buying and selling is carried out in a rather casual way on the pavements, in the main market, or in simply laid out shops jammed together along the ground floors of former colonial trading houses and more modern buildings. You will see numerous street hawkers, many of them from Senegal and Guinea, peddling sunglasses, counterfeit CDs, car steering wheel covers, auto air fresheners and other small items.

The best time to go sightseeing on foot to enjoy the architecture is after 5pm or on Saturdays and Sundays, when many businesses have closed for the day and private sector workers depart for the Kombos. Some of the oldest houses you might see are made of kirinting - bamboo weave houses covered in plaster and often painted with whitewash. These were often the homes of poorer African immigrants on Bathurst island constructed in the early part of the 19th century. Many were still built into the 20th century and can be found along Mam Mberry Njie Street, Essa Faal Street, McDonnel Street and James Senegal St. From around the 1830s came the next development in house style with the arrival of Christian Aku settlers from Freetown, Sierra Leone, to the island who introduced sturdier, Krio style wooden houses. Towards the end of the 19th century the French, Portuguese and British merchants built trading houses typically with wrought-iron colonnades at ground level and roofed balconies on the first floor that can still be seen along ECOWAS Avenue, Rene Blaine Street and Liberation Avenue.

On the north of the town is the Royal Victoria Teaching Hospital (RVTH), government ministries in the Quadrangle, law courts on Independence Drive and the new parliament building just past the Arch 22 on the highway leading out of the entrance to the capital. There are also a number of mosques in the capital. The first mosque was built in the 19th century called the Independence Drive Mosque, renamed the Masjid Abu Bakar Saddiq in 2014. Then there is the King Fahad Mosque, constructed in 1988 and named after Saudi Arabian King. It dominates the skyline at the north of the city and is one of Banjul's most recognisable landmarks.

Tourist Attractions & Things to Do:
Low-rise, often scorching, compact and teeming with mosquitoes in summer, it's not an instantly appealing place. Its concreted streets seem to exude

pulses of oppressive heat during the humid rainy season, with some smaller roads suffering occasional floods, which can prohibit leisurely shopping strolls and exploration around town. During the winter season it's an entirely different affair; a lot cooler and dryer, this is the time when most tourist visitors arrive with their tour operators or as independent travellers. The city however, is too compact to provide many of the expected amenities and diversions of a capital, and evening life is virtually unknown. The vast majority of workers leave the city after working hours and head south to their homes off of the island and onto the mainland districts of the Kombos. This maybe because from about the mid 1980s a gradual exodus of families out of the city and into the Kombos was well underway.

Arch 22

As you approach the end of the main highway leading into Banjul you will see to your right the rather futuristic looking parliament building. Then straight ahead is a roundabout with a statue of a soldier in the centre holding a small child, and above and behind is the Arch 22, which stands astride at the entrance to Independence Drive. Standing high at 35m it is a huge, cream-coloured, free-standing monument, built to commemorate the 22 July, 1994 bloodless coup when a young army officer, Yahya

Jammeh, took control of the country by ousting President Jawara. It offers great views over the city, coastal areas, the river and the mangroves of the Tanbi Wetland Complex. The skyline of Banjul is also graced by the twin minarets of the King Fahad Mosque and the State House, built by the Portuguese. On the top floor is a small museum housing ethnographic Gambian artifacts such a traditional textiles, agricultural tools and weapons such as bamboo bows and arrows and wooden swords.

Albert Market

One of the biggest tourists attractions in Banjul is the Royal Albert Market; it is a relaxed and oddly organised version of the everything-under-the-Sun style of market ubiquitous throughout West Africa. It is a maze of stalls and shops adequately spaced by paved walkways. Behind the main front façade, arcade, is two floors of numbered and roller-shuttered shops. On the top floor tailors work in booths side by side. In the first entrance alley you walk past the gauntlet of hawkers and ghetto blasters on both sides, giving you stereo music from different tracks.

Vegetable stallThe food stalls offer typical West African cooking ingredients such as yellow, orange and deep red chili peppers, tamarind, Okra (ladies fingers), bitter tomatoes, smoked catfish, very pungent, chopped and dried sea snails, dark palm oil, peanut past, a salted and dried pungent fish called 'gaija'. There are also seasonal fruits on display such as oranges, lemons, mangos, papaya and watermelons as well as imported apples and grapes. Groceries are sold in variable quantities, from rice by the cup full to cooking oil in 20 litre plastic bottle containers.

There are also stalls offering beauty products like shea butter, lipstick, hair-extensions, hand-made and imported soap, and household items of every kind such as buckets, cups, fans, flip-flops, sunglasses, perfumes, incense, fulano powder, traditional medicines, clocks, key-holders etc.

There are some good bargains to be had in clothing from the Far East, and fabrics such as wax prints, cottons and designed damask in vibrant colours. There is also a brisk trade in second-hand garments which arrive in Gambia mostly from Europe. You can find a number of fetish stalls, selling goat horns, loose cowrie shells, African trade beads, kola nuts and the aptly named bitter kola and much more.

As you go deeper into the market you will find the Banjul Tourist Craft Market (bengdula). There is a varied selection of batiks, leather goods, cheap and valuable jewellery such as bangles, silver necklaces and bracelets, djembe drums, etc. There are also a few stalls selling antiques such as wooden masks from the West Africa region.

Commercial Area

Albert Market spills out into the neighbouring road called Liberation Avenue and adjacent roads, where stores and stalls sell mostly cheaper, low quality clothing and footwear, plus a potpourri of household items and counterfeit CDs. There are also fabric importers who also distribute to the public on a retail basis, and offer an excellent range of imported fabrics in African and overseas designs. You can find many goods often sold at higher prices in Europe a lot cheaper in and around the market - as for quality the old doctrine of caveat emptor applies. Remember that as a general rule you need to try to haggle prices down by 30% to 40% lower than the initial asking price - 1/3 reduction is a good, general rule to remember. If you can't agree on a price then walk away, many will call you back, and that is a sign they are prepared to go lower, even if they don't say so immediately.

A worthwhile place to visit is the shop at the St. Joseph's Adult Education and Skills Centre. Based inside a colonial Portuguese building, the centre has provided skills training to disadvantaged women aged between 16 - 26 for over two decades. Here you can buy handmade clothes, knitted items, embroidered purses or take a tour of the of sewing, crafts and tie-dye classes. It is open weekdays in the mornings to early afternoons except for Friday when they close at mid-day.

Around the vicinity are banks and bureau de change, where you can change your foreign currency or your travellers' cheques, as well as some small but clean restaurants.

Gambia National Museum

The museum is in Banjul's northern sector on Independence Drive and was officially opened on 18th February, 1985. Within the pleasant front garden of tamarisk and palm there is a drinks stand and shaded seating area as well as toilets, administrative buildings and stores. The building used to house the Bathurst Club house consisting of European members only.

Even though it is quite small, cramped, and dimly lit, it contains some interesting, though sometimes not easy to find, artifacts - some a bit dog-eared, yearning for restoration. As you are about to enter the main hall you will see a Kankurang mask 'guarding' the door. Inside the display hall you will find numbered exhibits in a semblance of a circuit, from the late 19th and 20th centuries. You can find colonial era written and printed ephemera, including a passenger ticket from Bathurst to Liverpool on board the Elder Dempster Line's 'MV Apapa' - a so called a banana boat, bananas being one of the chief exports of the Gold Coast at the time. There is also a gathering of Oku marabout (Yoruba) pieces such as a bridal basket, waist beads called 'bin bin', an engagement calabash gourd, which would hold the bride's kola nuts, dowry and other oddments.

The museum also collects books, colonial maps, traditional music string instruments, cooking utensils such as large wooden mortars and pestles, large calabash gourds, Neolithic pottery, masks, the bau / worro (holed board game), handicrafts, large paper model boats called fanals, prehistoric tools, historical documents and photographs relating to the material culture of The Gambia. In some of the dimly lit corners, you'll see, among the crumbling ethnographic pieces, revealing old maps, papers and information about local migrations and conflicts in the Senegambia region, a few captivating pictures of kora players called jali, as well as masked dance ceremonies from an earlier era. Don't miss the life-sized Kankurang - a potent spirit incarnate, covered in baobab bark (from whom women, children and the uncircumcised must hide).

Bird Watching

If you are keen on birdwatching then head toward the most southerly road in the Banjul capital called the Kankujereh Road (Bund Rd.) which passes through bird rich saltwater wetland habitats with numerous bird species. It goes past the Gambia River estuary mudflats to your left with its rusting, mud sunken ships which are home to cormorants and pelicans roosts. At low tide, the mudflats are used as feeding grounds by striated herons, African spoonbills, gulls, waders and terns. To your right is some re-claimed land followed by the Tanbi Wetland Complex of mangroves to your right and left. Here you might spot black headed plover, yellow billed storks, little grebe, or the Senegal thick-knee. The best time to go is when there is light traffic such as after 11 am up to 5pm, but Fridays after 3pm and weekends are the best times to visit. Note: much of the area is strewn with scarp metal so sturdy boots and a stick might be useful.

Bird life

Sports Fishing

You could also go back towards the Denton Bridge and hire a local pirogue (long canoes - some with an outboard motor) which can take you out on the quiet waterways of Oyster Creek, which are rich fishing grounds for keen anglers. The dense mangroves are particularly interesting and home to around 70 species of fish and other wildlife such as tilapia, mullets, Atlantic mudskippers, shrimps, crabs and mangrove oysters. The fish fauna are of pelagic or demersal species in the fry, juvenile or sub-adult stages. You can also pick up a larger, more professional boat to take you up river or for some blue ocean sports fishing.

Restaurants & Nightlife

Banjul has an acute dearth of restaurants, especially in the evenings, but there is still some good quality basic food served from local diners and fast food establishments during the day. The Ali Baba Snack Bar serves European and Lebanese snacks, dishes, cold drinks, and freshly squeezed fruit juices. It's ideally located in the commercial district and close to the market and shops. On the same road is the King of Shawarma Cafe which has similar Middle Eastern cuisine plus dishes like fish & chips. If you feel the need to sit at a beach bar and restaurant facing the Atlantic ocean then try Nefertiti Beach Bar, just off the entrance of Marina Parade, near the Arch 22. It is at the end of the road leading past the registrar of companies and near the Atlantic Hotel; it is Lonely Planet's top choice among the places to eat.

There is virtually nothing in the capital city by way of night clubs as most people have left the town by 7pm, not to return until the next working day. The only night spot worth visiting for tourists is at the Atlantic Hotel, which is elegant, air conditioned, and opens till late. The people who do hang out in the evening are usually Gambians and foreigners, in front of their accommodation, drinking Attaya or visiting friends nearby, otherwise the streets are virtually empty. The only sounds you'll hear in the early evening are the various, distant calls of the muezzin, from minaret loudspeakers.

Other Attractions

MacCarthy SquareOther places to see in Banjul are the War Memorial & Fountain, near MacCarthy Square, erected to commemorate the coronation of Britain's King George VI in 1937. You can also visit MacCarthy Square which is surrounded by a colonial atmosphere, with eye-catching 19th-century architecture. It is used for public events such as Independence Day ceremonies, open concerts and cricket. There is also a children's playground with a modern play area which has colourful slides, swings, rocking horses and a small course.

Health & Safety:

Though a capital, Banjul has a typically relaxed small-town ambiance. If you have business to get on with, whatever you need to accomplish here can usually be done in relative safety - and at less than three square kilometres, the town can easily be crossed by foot. The police security presence, after the bridge crossing, is low-key. It's a town with individuals always on the move, so take the same safety precautions as in any urban area during the evenings. There is also a fire station in town.

Travel Information:

To get to the Banjul capital from the resorts takes about 20 minutes by car from the main resorts of Kololi and Kotu. The cost of a typical taxi fare for such a trip can vary between the cheaper yellow taxis and the more expensive green taxis.

When leaving the city there are two taxi ranks available: one is on the Independence Drive opposite the Gambia National Museum - if you want to go to Bakau, and the other is on the Mosque Road, with yellow cabs and assorted mini-vans going to Serrekunda (Westfield Junction) and Brikama Town. If you want more exclusive travel then ask for a 'Town Trip' to your destination. There are costlier green taxis outside the Atlantic Hotel. Having said all this you can pick up a cab anywhere, at any time, assuming they are empty and you wish to travel alone.

If you are going north across the Gambia River you can take the ferry service to Barra (7am to 11pm - tel no: 422 8205).

• Travel update: As at 27 December, 2014, the Bund Road (Kankujereh) has been closed for over one and a half years and is still undergoing resurfacing 'works'. Wallace Cole Road (Box Bar) is also still closed to traffic right up to Lasso Wharf, so the only traffic route into the heart of the capital is via Marina Parade, and onto Independence Drive.

Travel to Bakau

Introduction:
The Bakau resort is in the Kombo Saint Mary District, in the West Coast Region of The Gambia, and is the nearest holiday resort to the capital of Banjul which is 12km to the east. Bakau town includes the Cape Point promontory, and its northernmost coastline marks the point where the Atlantic Ocean meets the Gambia River. It is part desirable suburb, part shanty town and part coastal resort. The coastline is fringed with palm trees however, the beach area is composed of rocky, laterite cliff edges and at high tide the sand can disappear altogether. This is not

the case with Cape Point which descends onto a wide beach area.

Accommodation:

For travellers there are a number of basic hotels and guesthouses, and the town is a suitable if you are eager to lodge in the general area but not be to far away from the resort's beaches. Coming from the south the first hotel you will come across is the African Village Hotel which lies on the edge of a laterite cliff with a slither of beach at low tide. The Romana Afram Hotel is a small lodge at the edge of the town but on the main road called. The Garden Guest House is located in the heart of the gritty urban area. If you are looking for something more deluxe then you need to go further north to Cape Point which has a much better beach in a more genteel location.

GENERAL AREA:

Bakau Old Town

Local oral history says that the old village was established by the Bojang family over 500 years ago when crocodiles came and settled in what is now known as Katchikally. Today, along with the Sanchaba section, the Old Town is one of the oldest settlements in The Gambia. Among the first settlers to arrive were fishermen and their families. During the colonial era the locality was a desirable area for the British, and formed part of British Kombo which was basically the capital Banjul, Saint Mary's Island, and the outlying coastal areas to the west.

For holidaymakers, the Old Town's central points are the sections around the Atlantic Road junction, where it meets the Sait Matty Road. There is a post office, a few banks, a row of small bars and restaurants in front of the African Village Hotel, shops, a minimarket, Bakau Market and the tourist Craft Market (bengdula), where the Atlantic Boulevard meets the Cape Point Road. If you move a few metres inland you are in urban Gambia. A little to the south of the djembe drum producers and batik stands is the village marketplace.

The overcrowded residential area just inland is a tightly packed mish-mash of family compounds, sandy lanes, small shops, mechanic's workshops and so on. Over the years fishing families are being replaced by tourist sector workers. The residential neighbourhood, with its breeze block bungalows, rusting corrugated iron fences and smelly drainage ditches might not be everyone's cup of tea; however, there is virtually no traffic here so it's easier to travel around on foot than comparable areas in Serrekunda. Some of the densely populated backstreets have local diners, serving local food, which tend to be harder to find compared to the other resort areas.

Bakau New Town

The residential area of New Town is rich in mature trees that bloom into a riot of colour in the rainy season. Its main high street is the Garba Jahumpa Road (aka New Town Rd.) which connects the Sait Matty Road to the east, with the Kairaba Avenue's Fajara section to the west, locally known as the Sabena Junction (the place where Sabena Airline used to be based). The road is lined with small offices, clothing shops, minimarkets, tailors' workshops and private homes. It is very poorly lit at night and does not have much of a pavement to talk about. Not far from the centre point of this road is the Independence Stadium, the Gambia's national stadium. Built by the Chinese as a gift, it is a grand open-air venue surrounded by brush and a purpose built ring-road. The stadium is used for some major music concerts, July 22nd celebrations as well as football matches.

Tourist Attractions & Things to do:

Kachikally Crocodile Pool

Located on the southern section of the Old Town is the Kachikally Crocodile Pool. Local legend says it is a sacred pool which was later inhabited by crocodiles over 520 years ago. Its fresh waters are also said to be a treatment for infertility, bestow good fortune and occasionally certain rituals are held here, sometimes accompanies by drumming music. You can also visit a small ethnographic museum, a souvenir shop, a refreshment bar, all set in over 2.4 hectares of mini-forest which has a nature trail and is home to many tropical bird species, mammals, reptiles and insects.

Bird Watching
While you can find many bird species in Bakau's green areas, beaches and cliffs such as hooded vultures, Senegal coucal, Verreaux's eagle owl and the yellow-crowned gonolek. The best place for birdwatching is in the vicinity of Cape Creek in Cape Point. This area is largely made up of mangroves, mudflats, and sections of lightly wooded areas which are rich in various birds species.

Craft Market
For tourist shopping the Atlantic Boulevard's Craft Market is an ideal starting point. Here you can observe local craftsmen at work by the side of the road, under the shade of the trees. The bengdula has numbered stalls where you can find souvenirs such as African jewellery, batiks, wooden masks, tie-dye women's dresses, sand paintings, beads and more.

Bakau Botanical Garden

Located in Cape St. Mary, on the Old Cape Road, is the Botanical Garden, which was established in 1894. It is often missed by most tourists as it looks just like someone's large private front garden. It is set in an enclosed area within a link chain fence and there is a nature trail meandering around the trees as well as a grass shaded seating area called a Bantaba. Its plushest greenery can be seen towards the end of the rains in October. Specially worth noting among the labelled trees are the cycads, spiny, young silk cotton trees and the teak tropical hardwood. Only some of the shrubs and trees are indigenous, such as the rhun palms, and some need urgent pruning and care. If you come with a pair of binoculars you might be able to spot a number of bird species such as the red-cheeked cordon bleu, bronze mannikins or the odd bulbuls. It's a nice place to visit and relax in the afternoons and there is very little in the way of noise. The garden is open Monday to Saturday, 9 am till 5 pm, and there is an entrance fee of about £1.25 per person. Note: Apply mosquito repellent onto exposed areas of your body.

Bakau Village Market

Flies constantly make their way between make-shift stalls piled with habanero chili peppers, tomatoes and carrots, there are small hung yellow bags of cooking oil, chili powder, white rice, mounds of local fruit, used clothing, shoe stalls and lots shoddy, imported household products. You will also find bowls of fresh fish, beef and lamb on butcher's chopping boards and teeming with all manner of flies. The front of the market which is on the main road is lined with fruit and vegetable stalls selling tomatoes, guavas, bananas, oranges, apples and other fruits.

Bakau Fish Market & Jetty

On the other side of the road from the village marketplace is the beach fishing port of the local Fish Market where stalls can be found either near quayside or at the road side 100m from the taxi rank. At the bottom of a steeply sloped road you can see smokehouses as well as fish, such as bonga or butterfish, being brought onto the shore area from the brightly coloured African pirogues, the filleting process and ultimately the smoking or chilling and packing of the fish. You can buy fresh shrimps from next door to the taxi rank.

Other Points of Interest

There is the Gena Bes Batik & Tie Dye Batik Factory which has introduced modern designs that attracts higher-paying customers. 'Gena Bes' means 'newly out' in Wolof. Another place well worth looking at is the African Heritage Centre which is a combined art gallery and museum displaying and selling art objects from all over the country.

The local area is also home to the main military camp known as the Fajara Barracks, which is next door to the fire service, which in turn is about 50m to the local police station. Radio Gambia is also located here on the road heading towards Sting Corner and the capital of Banjul in an area called Mile Seven.

Health & Safety:
The general area along the coastal strip is the safest place in The Gambia, given the presence of a large number of professional security guards, local watchmen, the military barracks, the police station and numerous residences occupied by international organisation workers. Safety and security is very good between the army camp and Kofi Annan Street in Cape Point, where the road is also lit.

Travel Information:
To get to the heart of Bakau ask one of the drivers of the yellow or green tourist taxis to take you to the local taxi rank next to the fish landing harbour, and you can start your sightseeing trip from there. To get back to your hotel (if you are staying in Kololi or Kotu) just pick up a cab from in front of the nearby Trust Bank building which is near the African Village Hotel.

Travel to Bijilo

Introduction:

The Bijilo resort and Bijilo village are in the West Coast Region of the Kombo North St. Mary District (Ksmd), of The Gambia, in West Africa, and are 23km southwest of the capital of Banjul. The old village and its new residential areas are about 2 km south of Kololi and the Senegambia Strip area, and are mostly to the right of the Bertil Harding Highway, while the resort includes the village and much of the area to the left of the road, facing the Atlantic Ocean. This section of the coast is more peaceful than its seafront counterparts to the north, and there are far fewer bumsters.

Accommodation:

This section of the coastal strip and the inland neighbourhood of Kerr Serign are relatively late comers as holiday resorts. The accommodation choices are tranquil and sparsely spaced. However, it is an important growth area, and available seaside plots are being taken up quickly, and construction of new places to stay continues apace. The hoteliers here are mostly aiming at the top-spending end of the tourism sector. Among the places to stay are the tourist-class Lemon Creek, Golden Beach Hotel and Bijilo Beach Hotel, the luxury Coco Ocean Resort &

Spa, the deluxe self-catering Sea Front Residence and other hotels.

Beach Area:

Back in the 1970s the beach area was a quiet backwater of the Gambia's Kombos. It was characterised by a covering of dense, closed woodland, dominated by rhun palms with some coconut trees, and its shore were virtually deserted. Today, much of the woodland south of Bijilo Forest Park has been thinned to make way for tourist related industries and private homes. The area's beaches are still relatively quiet, save for the sections facing the hotels. Between the gaps of the various accommodations are a few bars and restaurants. The sands are golden, wide and clean, and make an excellent place for sunbathing and, when the sea is calmer, for swimming. It is also common to see vervet monkeys in the general area, sometimes they visit bars to titbits of food. Sometimes you can see Serer fishermen landing their catches on shore from their pirogues. The area along the main Kombo Coastal Road, parallel to the Atlantic strip, is well lit and foot access to the ocean side is quite good.

When the sun sets, Bijilo is at its best. The palm trees are wrapped in a red glow and the green bushes stand out so vividly that they dazzle the eyes. A herd of cows is driven slowly along the beach by a small boy; their dun colour and soft lowings add to the beauty of the peaceful scene..."

General Area:

The sleepy village of Bijilo has undergone gentrification, as the old farming families have largely sold up and moved out. Modern residential homes and highway office blocks, shops and lodges are rapidly replacing the fields and old structures of the village. Well spaced sandy streets separate bungalows and villas with pools.

Tourist Attractions & Things to Do:

1. Restaurants

There are a few decent restaurants here such as the following:

2. Bamboo Beach Bar (International cuisine)

3. Jaama Bar (Local seafood)

4. Kasumai (International cuisine)

5. La Pirogue

6. Sunbird Bar & Restaurant

7. Quad Biking

Quad bikeThis way of exploring the beaches and and further afield is increasingly popular. You can often rent a quad bike from the beachfront itself. Also ask at the reception as they may know about a few firms engaged in quadbiking hire. Check that your holiday insurance policy covers this mode of transport. There is a safari tour operator that specializes in quad biking on a set rout called West African Powersports.

1. Horseback Riding

Horses for hire can be found along most of the beachfronts in Gambia and is a different way of exploring sections of the coast quickly, and getting some refreshing sea air into your lungs. Sometimes they are kept by the hotels themselves. Again, just ask at the reception desk for information.

2. Sunbathing & Swimming

Bijilo is one of the few beachfronts along this section of the 10.5km strip where you can sunbath in peace and quiet. Keep an eye out for swimming conditions according to the lifeguard's flags. The sand is soft, clean and wide enough so you can keep out of the way of 'beach traffic' such as horse riders and cows!

Health & Safety:

In and around the built up areas is quite safe and the main road is usually lit at night. If you want to veer off into the village at night then, for your own safety, do not go unaccompanied, and carry a small torchlight with you as the side streets are not lit, except by lights from family compounds and shops.

Travel Information:
There are no obvious spots to pick up a taxi on this part of the Bertil Harding Highway, but they are constantly plying the road for business so you won't have to wait too long. You can travel out-and-about from your accommodation by hiring one of the green taxis parked near the entrance of the major hotels

Travel to Brufut

Introduction:
The Brufut resort and village (also known as Burfut or Burufut) is between the Atlantic Ocean and the coastal forest, in Kombo South District, West Coast Region of The Gambia in West Africa, and is 23km by road to Banjul capital and 7km south from Kololi. The old village is about 1.5 kilometres to the east of the Kombo Coastal Road and has spread westward to the beachfront to include Brufut Heights holiday resort and Brufut Gardens residential community. The other nearby area is Ghana Town founded by Ghanaian fishermen many years ago.

Accommodation:

This section of the coastal region has undergone rapid development over the years, a number of hotels have sprung up to cater for the increased demand for accommodation located away from the tourist holiday hotspots of Senegambia Strip and Kotu. In March 2007, the beach based Sheraton 5 Star Hotel Resort (now the Coral Beach Hotel) was finally completed and opened for guests. You will find a number of quiet lodges and guest houses located on the seaside such as the deluxe, boutique hotels called Leo's Beach Hotel and the Ocean Villa Heights. Further inside the village itself boutique hotel called Hibiscus House, the much praised, down to Earth boutique lodge called The Plantation.

Taf Estate photoThere is also the private, fenced and gated housing community called the TAF Brufut Gardens Estate, with its modern bungalows, apartments and villas starting on the coastal road itself. The estate is popular with expatriates and Gambians living abroad who are looking to purchase a house that is near the beach.

Beach Area:
The Brufut beach area is fairly wide with nice golden sands. To get to the beach you would need to make your way down the rust coloured cliffs dotted with trees and bushes using fairly steep paths. At the palm tree fringed beachfront you might see African

pirogues parked on the sand, waiting for the tide to change, women separating fish and fishermen repairing their nets. Away from these places, the beaches are almost deserted, say for a few children playing or the occasional villager using it as a short-cut. You can use these sections of the strand for watersports, cycling or sunbathing.

General Area:

Brufut village is an old settlement of block compounds with corrugated metal roofs, resided by mostly Mandinka farmers and vegetable plots. Increasingly however, land is being sold to private individuals and estate developers due to the high demand for plots to build housing space. To get to the original village you take the part laterite, part dirt road east for a few kilometres. During the rainy season this road is often dotted with pools of water which is best suited for four wheel drive cars.

The Atlantic coastal road has seen the installation of road lights running all the way from the AU Highway at Brusubi Turntable, and south just short of Ghana Town. Nawec (the electrical utilities firm) has also laid mains water and electricity cables that follow the coastal road and are being extended to private homes.

Tourist Attractions & Things to Do:

Bird Watching

The Brufut Woods Community Project is a locally managed conservation area in partnership with the West African Bird Study Association (WABSA). It is located on the eastern periphery of the village, some way inland, over some rough back routes. The small nature reserve has a birdwatching hide specially placed near to an artificial pond. One of the best places in the woods is an open area near the bridge.

The resident and inter-African migrant bird species you might see among the gallery forest and open savannah woodland are the Pin-Tailed Whydahs, Black Crowned Tchagra, African Scops Owls, Black Kite, Klaas's Cuckoo, Emerald Cuckoo, Senegal Batis, Osprey, Scarlet-chested Sunbird, Verreaux's Eagle Owl, Fork-Tailed Drongo, Four-banded Sandgrouse and the Yellow-throated Leaflove.

Sanneh-Mentering

This is a holy, sacred site, a more scenic and evocative place of pilgrimage. A short stroll south from the Sheraton (preferably accompanied by a knowledgeable person from the community) brings you to the cliff-top clearing, overlooking the beach, with its huge baobab tree and simple hut in a grove. The stone at the base of the tree is for alms: kola-nuts, money, cloth. The air is filled with the smell of incense burned by the incumbent marabout.

Muslims from all over The Gambia come here for good fortune, a more profitable business, health cures or pray here at a time of crisis in their lives. Women also come here for a special wash from well water at the bottom of the cliff, in the hope of overcoming infertility. (The place is also spelt Sanamentering, Sannehmentering, Sanimentereng or Sanementereng).

Restaurants & Beach Bars
There are a number of coastal beach bars such as Village's Beach Bar, Pelican Bar, Dolphin, Ocean Blue Beach Bar & Restaurant, Sibis Garden (Chatty's) and Leo's Hotel Twins Beach Bar serving serving fish domoda with rice, fish in foil with onions, Barracuda or Ladyfish with rice or chips. They also have juices and Julbrew beer.

Health & Safety:
The area is safest along the resort's coastal road. Do not venture into the village on foot alone at night, and do carry a small torchlight and money belt or pouch.

Travel Information:
Some mini-buses and yellow taxis travel south into Brufut from Kololi and Fajara taxi ranks. You will have to change get off at Brusubi Turntable, and take another taxi towards Brusubi.

Travel to Cape Point

Introduction:

The Cape Point beach resort makes up the north-eastern part of the town of Bakau, in the Kombo St Mary District, in the West Coast Region of The Gambia, and is 12km to the west of Banjul capital. The district is a promontory and its beach area is where the River Gambia and the Atlantic Ocean merge at the estuary. To Cape Point's eastern coastline is a wide seafront of fine, golden sand, while much of its north-western coastline starts at sea level, then, as you head south west it rises up to over 15 metres, and is mostly characterised by laterite cliffs dotted with palms along a narrow strand. Further to its southeast are the brackish mangrove swamps of Cape Creek, frequented by wetland birds.

Accommodation:

The tourist enclave is in a very quiet part of town and close to a scenic seafront, which is fringed by hotels, palm trees, bushes, and up-market private residences. There are a number of smaller hotels and guesthouses offering budget accommodation such as the Cape Point Hotel. The main tourist-class hotels here are the Ocean Bay Hotel & Resort and the Sunbeach Hotel & Resort. If you prefer self-catering in deluxe surroundings with a small shared pool, then try one of the 12 luxury holiday apartments of the Cape Residence.

Beach Area:

Cape Point beach and its adjacent area is one of The Gambia's most family-friendly holiday resorts, and here the wide, beautiful strip of sand is lined with mature palm trees, grasses and thatched sunshades. You might also see some basalt boulders strategically place along part of the shoreline to counteract erosion of the sands. Although erratic currents make it unsuitable for swimming, it's perfect for sunbathing, volleyball, strolling, picnics, and making sandcastles, and there's a broad choice of restaurants and beach bars close by. In the country as a whole there are often sightings of roaming livestock, so don't be surprised if you see the odd goat or cow trudging along the sand roaming and looking for anything edible to eat. There are also juice stands near the southern part of the main strand selling various juices such as mango, melon, coconut, baobab, orange and grapefruit.

Sundays is the main day when local Gambians come to the strand to relax with their families or play a bit of football or volleyball.

General Area:

Not only is the district's shore area a tourist magnet it is also an exclusive residential location which has a large number of people from the diplomatic community, such as Britain's diplomatic residence, 'Admiralty House', well-to-do businessmen, politicians and some well established family compounds. The vast majority of these homes are within the triangle formed by the Kofi Annan Street, the Old Cape Road and Capepoint Road.

At the tourist centre is the tourist craft market, several bureau de change, mini-markets, some bars and restaurants and green tourist taxis; all accompanied by a high level of security provided by security guards and official paramilitary police. This makes the general locality the safest place to live or go on holiday. Furthermore, the water and electricity supplies are more stable here and you are less likely to experience power outages.

A Little History:

Ocean Bay HotelThe promontory was 'discovered' by Portuguese navigators of this part of West Africa in the 15th century, and they named it 'Cabo de Santa Maria' (Cape of Saint Mary). The name overflowed to the nearby island when the British established the capital Bathurst (now Banjul). It was part of 'British Kombo' in the mid 1800s.

Tourist Attractions & Things to Do:

Birdwatching

The most fruitful areas for birdwatching are around Cape Creek, which is traversed by the Old Cape Road southeast of Bakau, and Sting Corner, at the intersection of Sait Matty Road and the Serrekunda to Banjul Highway. The road that cuts through the creek is a pleasurable stroll at any time of day during the winter season, going past a thinly wooded area of baobab trees, oil palm trees, tamarisk, tall grasses and rhun palms. The Creek is surrounded by swamp mangroves and brackish mudflats; this sector produces sightings of many bird species such as parakeets, marsh harriers, blue-bellied rollers, gull-billed and Caspian terns, blue-cheeked bee-eaters, black kites, blue-breasted kingfishers and starlings; while the mudflats are frequented by birds such as the Senegal thick-knees and spur-winged plovers. In the creek you may see fish-eating birds such as ospreys, reef herons, pied kingfishers, long-tailed shags and red-chested swallows.

Red chested swallow

While on route from Bakau to Sting Corner via Sait Matty Road you will see the vegetable gardens tended to by the Bakau Women's Cooperative, and, especially in the rice growing season, this is an excellent place to spot cattle egrets, lily-trotters and squacco herons.

Crocodile Pool

The lagoon was initially cut into the sands by the ocean and is in front of the Calypso Restaurant. The lagoon was then expanded and made more permanent when the Gambian owner of the diner found a few West African crocodiles had decided to make it their home. It is now partly lined with large laterite rocks and grasses, and has become a local tourist attraction for holidaymakers and locals alike. In fact as you head south towards the creek there is an increased likelihood of seeing wild crocodiles among the vegetation.

Craft Market

Called the Sunwing Tourist Craft Market it is located on a road island occupying half of one side. There are numbered shop units selling a variety of souvenirs such as batiks, tie & dye hangings, wooden carved masks, necklaces, drums, necklaces, shoes and trade beads. Nearby you can find women selling a variety of tropical fruits from their street side stalls.

Horse Riding

It is possible to do some horseback riding on Cape Point's strand which are available from the Ocean Bay and Sunbeach hotels. Often you will find them exercising their horses up and down the beachfront; all you have to do is stop one of them and ask the price for a session.

Botanical Gardens

Tropical palmsThe Bakau Botanical Garden is situated just after the end of the northern point of Atlantic Road and was established in the last decade the 19th century. The trees and shrubs are surrounded by a fence and is signposted on the main road. There is a walking track that works its way around the garden's labelled trees as well as a grass roofed shaded area to sit in and relax. It is at its most green towards the end of the monsoon season. There are also an assortment of bird species fluttering between the trees and you might be lucky to spot a bulbul or mannikin among others.

Health & Safety:

The Cape Point enclave is renowned in The Gambia for the high level of security and safety due to the presence of numerous security personnel working in this largely residential area. Starting from the Craft Market the Atlantic Road is well lit but provides little in the way of a pedestrian pavement, while Kofi Annan Street is also well lit, wider and has access to the beach from the Ocean Bay Hotel. Going along the Old Cape Road towards Banjul the road is lit but bordered by mangroves, and it is not recommended to walk along here at night. There is plenty of vegetation in the area harbouring mosquitoes, particularly straddling the beach, so do apply sufficient mosquito repellent at dusk to reduce your chances of getting malaria.

Travel Information:

Despite not being a major through route there are yellow (standard) and green tourist taxis constantly in the area around the Sunwing Craft Market to take you to the nightspots in places such as Kololi and Kotu. The are sometimes bicycles for rent near the Ocean Bay Hotel and is a good way to explore the general area and the creek as well as ride south towards Bakau and Fajara. Car rentals are available from some of the larger tourist hotels.

Travel to Fajara

Introduction:

BeachThe Fajara resort and residential town is in the Kombo Saint Mary District, Greater Banjul area, in the West Coast Region of The Gambia, West Africa, and lies 14km east of the Banjul capital. The coastal suburb is a tranquil, relatively prosperous residential neighbourhood, taking in about half of Kairaba Avenue, eastward inland, almost up to Latrikunda.

The area is officially divided into sections called 'M' Section, 'F' Section and 'A' Section. The western part towards the Atlantic coast is called Fajara 'M' Section; many of The Gambia's finest restaurants and stores are located there. Compared to Bakau, the 'M Section' district has a unique character, with sleepy neighbourhoods and sandy roads often lined with grand villas, partially hidden by tall block fences often draped in flowers.

Accommodation:
The holiday room options in Fajara are usually great value small hotels, lodges and guest houses, with added charm and character that's often missing in the other resorts. The nearest thing to a tourist-class hotels here are the seafront based, luxury Ngala Lodge which has a pool, a fine restaurant and excellent bedrooms and suites. The other is the Fajara Hotel, which is on the beachfront, and is the largest accommodation with fantastic vistas of the Atlantic Ocean and coastline. There is a small lodgings called the Safari Garden, which has a pool and a family friendly atmosphere, located in the heart of the residential district and only 10 minutes walk to the Leybato beach.

Beach area:
Fajara's beaches are comprised of two types. Starting north from the African Village Hotel in Bakau, and

southwards just after Ngala Lodge, the width of the sand is very narrow or at high-tide non-existent. This portion of the coast is dominated by red laterite cliffs, boulders, dense cliff top rhun palms, trees and narrow lanes, but offer fantastic views of the Atlantic Ocean South and coastline. As you head further south, the resort's strand becomes much wider and sandier heading towards Kotu Strand, and offers plenty of opportunities for sunbathing, shopping at the craft market, watersports like beach volleyball, or a a pleasant early morning or evening stroll.

If you want to swim in the sea do first look out for swimming conditions warming flags put up by the attendant lifeguards. Do not attempt to sunbath on the narrow strip of sand just off the cliff areas as you could fall asleep while the tide is rising. It would be much easier to just walk along the shoreline, southwards, or take a taxi to the Golf Course road and make you way down the small, paved path to the seashore.

General Area:
Fajara is first and foremost a residential district, housing prosperous businessmen, diplomats, local politicians and early settling Gambian families. The quality of the houses does vary given that people began to settle here many decades ago, and as a result buildings were constructed at different times.

There are comfortably spaced bungalows and large new villas in amongst the quiet sandy lanes with the occasional corner shop, small restaurant and hairdressers making an appearance.

The main thoroughfare is the Kairaba Avenue which starts at the coast, and has good taxi links. The 'M' section of the road is lined with fine boutiques, diners, office blocks, international banks, supermarkets, clothing stores, hardware retailers and other kinds of shops.

Tourist Attractions & Things to Do:

Africa Living Art Centre
It is located on the Fajara end of the Garba Jahumpa Road, in the lower part of Bakau New Town, the Africa Living Art Centre is a one-of-a-kind building in Gambia. Designed by its owner, it is a tree shaded, two storey, decorated glass and concrete gallery which itself resembles an impressive work of art. Filled with a colourful, diverse collection of exhibits and merchandise such as West African antiques, jewellery, ritual wooden masks and some of the most unique and imaginative garments to be found anywhere in the country. Also on display are paintings by Mr. Suelle Nachif, some showing the hallowed kanaga sign of the Dogon people of Mali.

He also hosts workshops, exhibitions and brings artists together.

The space inside has a hair salon, book library area, and the YOK bar cafe, and is a nice place to eat various snacks such as sandwiches, pastries, Lebanese coffee or refreshing soft drinks and cocktails.

Bird Watching

The best birdwatching spots in Fajara are at the Golf Course and the slope from there leading down to the shore. With the Kotu stream flowing near part of the course plus some woodland patches and coastal scrub this area provides a range of habitats for a number of bird species. Here you might be able to spot Abyssinian Rollers, Blue-bellied Roller, Bearded Barbets, Black-headed Plovers, Red-billed Godwits, Senegal Thick-knee, Firefinches, Blue-cheeked Bee-eaters, Variable Sunbirds and Beautiful Sunbirds.

Club & Golf Course

The sports club, formerly known as the Bathurst Club, transferred from Banjul to its current premises in July 1955; being the old headquarters of the long defunct BOAC airline's hall on south Atlantic Road. The Fajara Club is best known for its 18-hole golf-course (par 69) near the beach, having moved from its former location at Denton Bridge many decades ago. Don't expect to see much 'green' on the lawns during the dry season; more dry grass and fine sand than lush lawns of Bahama grass.

With the clubs main rooms in an old colonial era building, it's not instantly appealing. But it's more than made up for by the sports and recreational facilities available, such as tennis courts with floodlights, a badminton hall, squash courts, a swimming pool and table tennis. There is also a fitness gym, yoga classes and aerobics. Basic meals and drinks are reasonably priced and served from the clubhouse bar (Tel no: 4495456).

There is a group called the Hash House Harriers who meet there and who organise runs and walks about once a week (Tel no: 4495054).

Restaurants
There are a handful of excellent restaurants within the residential roads of Fajara, as well as on the main highway cutting through the resort. If you are on a budget you can still have an enjoyable meal as some of the no frills diners. Below is a selection of some of the well known diners in the area.

1. Koko Curry (Indian cuisine)

2. Butcher's Shop Restaurant (Moroccan)

3. Francisco's Restaurant (International & local cuisine)

4. Mama's Bar & Restaurant (European & African)

5. Ngala Lodge (The diner is open to public; best international cuisine)

6. Clay Oven (Indian dishes)

7. Shopping

Starting a few metres from the US Embassy and going along Kairaba Avenue towards the Atlantic coast, you will find dozens of retail stores lining the road. The shops here however are not geared towards tourist trinkets and souvenirs, they are aimed more at relatively affluent locals who are looking to buy food, clothes, furniture etc. If your travel budget can stretch a bit then try and visit the Emporium Shopping Centre. It is a vast glass and marble effect facade building, selling top quality imported home furnishings such as vases, tables, sheets, chairs, curtain fabrics, ornaments and other merchandise. The Emporium also has a gift shop and store with bodycare products. There are plenty of small items that you can pick up while on holiday and keep within your baggage allowance.

Tourist Craft Market is on Fajara beach, near to Kotu Strand. Here you can buy African jewellery, brightly coloured batiks, drums, wood carvings, sandals, tie and dye, handbags and more. To reach here you go down to the end of the Atlantic Road, near the Golf Course entrance, and take the small footpath to your right, which goes all the way down to the seafront.

The Timbooktoo Bookshop is a 3-storey megabookstore on the Garba Jahumpa Road, not far from the Sabena junction at Kairaba Avenue. It has a superb choice of non-fiction and fiction, including a wealth of African literature by Africans, plus periodicals, stationery and local newspapers. Inside is the Mango Cafe. Timbooktoo also has the Cultural Encounters Information Centre where tourists can enquire about local lodgings, ground tours and other travel information for people on holiday to The Gambia.

If you need groceries, bodycare products, toiletteries, small housewares, especially if you are in nearby self-catering accommodation, there is the well stocked mini-market called the Discount Centre. They have a good range of cereals, milk, yoghurt, biscuits, potato chips, soft drinks and much more. They also have a few clothes in their expanded section.

a) Landmarks

Among the well known landmarks in Fajara M Section are the American Embassy Banjul, Emporium Shopping Mall, Sankung Sillah Building, Galp Energia Petrol Station, Standard Chartered Bank building and the Traffic Lights Junction.

b) War Cemetery

The Fajara War Cemetery has 203 people interred there, 4 of which are unidentified. It includes Gambian, British and Canadians who lost their lives in World War 2. It is maintained by the Commonwealth War Graves Commission and includes a RWAFF memorial tablet dedicated to local servicemen buried overseas.

Health & Safety:

The resort area here is quite a safe place to stay for travellers to The Gambia. The incidence of serious crime is very low, and there are security personnel and local watchman in over 90% of the residential properties here, and the main roads are usually well lit.

When walking along this end of Kairaba Avenue avoid walking on the road itself. Vehicles often overtake each other here and you could place yourself at risk of injury. If you are dining out in the evenings do rub on mosquito repellent on your arms, neck and legs, if exposed. Finally, whenever you feel thirsty while out and about buy bottle water as opposed to the sachets. These are sometimes contaminated and their source is sometimes dubious. Finally, the nearest fire station is in Bakau.

Travel Information:

In the 'M Section' there is a yellow taxi rank on the Bertil Harding Highway (opposite the Galp Petrol Station). A cab there can take you down towards Kololi, Senegambia, and beyond to Bijilo, Kerr Serign and Brusubi. There are no minibuses at the rank but do drive past, so you can hail one from the street. There is also a small taxi rank at the coastal end of Atlantic Road, very near to Francisco's Bar & Restaurant.

The regular travel routes taken by vans is from the Bakau Village Market, down Sait Matty Road, down the Garba Jahumpa Road and onwards to Serrekunda along the Kairaba Avenue. To get to Fajara from Banjul International Airport you can hire a taxi (green). It will cost about a third more than yellow taxis, but the yellow cabs aren't allowed to wait at the airport. Outside the airport the fares are posted up on the right side of the main entrance on your way out. If you need to hire a self-drive vehicle from the airport then try Hertz Rent A Car.

The other mode of local transport is by rickshaw. You will have to flag them down.

Travel to Gunjur

Introduction:
Gunjur Village and Gunjur beach resort, are in the Kombo South District, of the West Coast Region, in the southwest coastal strip of The Gambia, in West Africa. It has an estimated population of 27,000 made up of mostly Mandinka, Jola, Fula, Manjago, Balanta, Karoninka and other ethnic groups, mainly employed in artisanal fisheries and farming. The settlement is 10 kilometres from Sanyang and 39 kilometres by road from the capital of Banjul. About 3km from the main town, and on the coast, is the bustling fishing village with its fish smoking houses and rows of multi-coloured African pirogues. North of the fish centre, the beaches are excellent for miles.

Accommodation:
Despite the locality's relative remoteness it has a respectable selection of good quality seafront resorts and inland travellers' lodgings. If you really want peace and quiet then go for the coastal hotels and lodges such as Nemasu Eco-Lodge, a unique and

Earthy retreat, combining traditional and modern in 8 huts, a clean place on the sands. The Footsteps Eco-Lodge is set some distance from the beach but has a natural swimming pool and well honed services with 9 huts. There is also the The Gunjur Project Lodge with its 8 chalets. All the above have ensuite bathing and WC. This part of Gambia is great for camping backpackers.

Beach Area:

The seafront area of Gunjur resort is, at most times, gloriously deserted, save for the odd passing cow and the occasional passerby. The strand is less geared to tourist than some of the northern holiday resorts and there are a few dotted beach bars and lodges nestled on the edge of huge rhun palm clusters and shoreline bush. Pristine yellowish sand sweeps the edges of broad bays, presenting impressive views into the distant shoreline, and the sunsets are magnificent. In terms of natural beauty, this region's seafront perhaps only comes second to Sanyang, located further north.

General Area:

The village is a tranquil, sleepy quarter, with dirt roads and simple block-work abodes topped with corrugated sheets. The community is well served with good paved road connections along the coast and a highway leading up to Brikama town; the taxi rank is located in the edge of town. There are a few stores, diners and a couple of mini-markets in town and the village is now connected to the water and electricity utilities.

Outside the settlement are large and small farm field holdings, woodland scrub, some forest and dotted with a few private residential homes. Between the main village and the Atlantic Ocean is thick tropical palm forest, dry woodland, coastal scrub, mangroves, a coastal lagoon, baobab trees, acacia and cashew orchards riddled with dirt roads.

There are various NGOs working in the rural and urban community such as the Trust Agency For Rural Development (TARUD), the Gunjur Environmental Protection & Development Group (GEPADG), and the Marlborough Brandt Group (the village is twinned with the town of Marlborough in UK).

Founding Family History:
Oral history suggests that the first people to settle in Gunjur were the Sanyang family who are Bianunkas of the Biyaro tribe. It is said they established a small settlement close to an Atlantic coastal lagoon called Bolong Fenyo. According to a colonial commissioner's note of 1941, the village was founded by the Darboe family, who were pagans who migrated from Manding (Mali) hundreds of

years ago and obtained permission from the kings of Brikama to make this area of land their home. Their site was nearer to the sea than the present village in what is today known as Senga Forest. Some time later they were joined by the Tourays from Futa Toro, and the Sahos.

Tourist Attractions & Things to Do:

Gunjur Fishing Village

Visiting the largest fisheries centre in Gambia, at Bator Sateh, at the end of the Beach Road, is one of the best ways to experience vibrant village life. In what would appear to be smoke-filled organised chaos at the harbour, you can see brightly painted, multi-coloured African longboats heave, sway and surge on the often threatening Atlantic Ocean waves. Women sometimes wade in shoulder high to collect the catch in wide plastic buckets on their heads. Once the pirogues are on shore they are then manually hauled in on chunky wooden rollers to the shouts of fishery workers. The fish catch, often bonga, is traded by fishmongers, sometimes gutted and washed, then dried, frozen or smoked in dim, hazy, rusting sheds and pungent cold stores, while fishing nets are mended and pirogue hull breaches repaired. Most of the fishermen are Senegalese, many of whom live in the town.

Gunjur Village Museum

Located in Babilon, the initiative to build the Cultural Heritage Museum came from Lamin Bojang in 2008, while working at the Footsteps Eco-Lodge. The small museum, which is now registered with National Centre for Arts and Culture (NCAC), aims to preserve the areas oral historical accounts, culture and artifacts. Among the ancient and more modern pieces on exhibit are intricately carved   human figurines, wooden stools and bowls, carved wooden masks, decorated bino horns, clay water containers, hot press irons, metal cooking pots, musical instruments like the Kora and Balafon.

Koofung Private Forest Park

Located to the west of the Kombo Coastal Road this is a small nature reserve where you can see various bird species and animals such as green vervet monkeys and other wildlife.

Bolong Fenyo Community Wildlife Reserve

The 345 hectares of protected coastal and marine park called Bolong Fenyo is managed by the Gunjur Environmental Protection & Development Group (GEPADG bnbajo@gmail.com   Tel no: 8800986 / 4486001). You can contact them for a tour of the wildlife park, and gain some good community insights into how it combines the preservation of the area's delicate biodiversity to local job creation, and can organise cultural dance performances and food. For birdwatchers, their focus of interest would be the coastal lagoon, a site that draws in over 75 recorded bird species (some claim to have seen 119), including Double-banded Sandgrouse, Green Crombec and Little Crake. There are also reptiles, snakes, mammals and invertebrates such as humpback dolphins and green turtles.

Bird Watching

Visitors to Gunjur who fancy doing a bit of birdwatching can find numerous bird species in variable habitats. Among these are the African Spoonbill, Hybrid Red Bellied X African Paradise Flycatcher, Red-billed Firefinch, Lavender Waxbill, Brown Babbler, Vinaceous Dove, Pied-winged Swallow, Common Bulbul, Abyssinian Roller, Bronze mannikin, Spur-winged Lapwing, Western Red-billed Hornbill, Village Weaver, African Pygmy Kingfisher, Black Heron, Western Grey Plantain-eater, Wire-tailed Swallow, Black-winged Red Bishop, Piapiac, Red-cheeked Cordon-bleu, Laughing Dove, Spur-winged Plover, Senegal Firefinch, Striped Kingfisher, Variable Sunbird, Western Bluebill, African Thrush, Black-necked Weaver, Grey-headed Gull, Yellow-crowned Gonolek, Snowy-crowned Robin-Chat, Blue-bellied roller, Senegal Parrot, Western Bluebill and Purple Glossy Starling.

Sports Fishing

Shore angling can be quite rewarding among the Gunjur coastline's shallow reefs, sandy bays and rocky outcrops. With the right rod and tackle you might snag Barracuda, Catfish, Guitarfish (Shovel-nosed Rays), Captain Fish, Butterfish, Stingrays, various Croakers, and Red or Guinean snappers from the seafront. Shore fishing is good throughout the year, at high or low tide.

Surfing

'Secret Bay' has been deemed suitable for all levels of surfers by wannasurf.com. Waves have an estimated swell size of 1m / 3ft and holds up to 2m+ / 6ft+ and a frequency of 150 days a year, with a good day length of 50 to 150m. The bay is located south of the coastal fish landing site, between Bator Sateh and Gunjar Madina.

About 1km from Gunjur's main fishing centre is a sacred site called the Sand Dune Mosque, or Kenye-Kenye Jamango ('Mosque soil' in Mandinka), which overlooks a spectacular sweep of beachfront from a high dune. Made famous by a visit here by the much revered Sheikh Umar Futiu Taal in the late 1830s. He had thousands of loyal followers and had imposed his authority from Senegal to Nigeria. The palm-frond mosque, and associated grounds, such as rocks and buildings are all considered sacred, and some pilgrims have been known to stay for up to one year here. A half mile south of here is Tengworo ('6 Palm Trees') where recently circumcised boys are bathed. North of Kenye-Kenye is Nyanitama-Dibindinto, a holy place of prayer where infertile women make offerings in the hope of conceiving. If you want to visit any of these sacred places you should be accompanied by a knowledgeable local guide. Note that non-Muslims are not allowed to enter the mosque.

Health & Safety:

When staying in the rural area beware of animal as well as possible human risks. There are a few poisonous snakes in the bushy areas such as cobra, therefore it's advisable to always wear boots when trekking in the scrub. During the evenings it's best to stay within close proximity of your lodgings, and if you have to go some distance then to only go out at night by car and accompanied. If you are camping on the beach or remote locality, then do be aware of your personal safety when on the coast at night. Use the services of a tourist guide and get advise from one of the local organisations. Finally, don't drink water straight from the tap. Drink purified water, use a portable water filter or sterilizations tablets. If possible bring along plenty of insect repellent, preferred toiletries and sun block cream.

Travel Information:

Gunjur can be reached by taking one of the yellow normal taxis or one of the four wheel drive green tourist taxis from the northerly resorts of Kololi and Kotu, and travelling south along the Kombo Coastal Road, it is about 10 km after Sanyang. To get back to your hotel go to the taxi rank on the outskirts of the village, and consider taking a shared bush taxi (van) all the way to Brusubi, then take a cab from there. This last trip can be reversed making it the cheapest option of travel.

If you are visiting this area then do pack plenty of your most essential supplies. There are some mini-markets now open in town

Travel to Jinack Island

Introduction:

Jinack Island (also spelt Jinak or Ginak) is in the North Bank Region of the Lower Niumi District of The Gambia, in West Africa. It is located on the north western edge of the River Gambia estuary, and is separated from the mainland delta of the Niumi National Park by the Niji Bolon creek. The isle, often referred to by tour operators as 'Paradise Island' or 'Treasure Island', is a slightly curved and tapering strip of low-lying land about 10km long; with an interior of dry woodland and grassland, with vegetation such as Tamarisk scrub, baobab trees and acacia. It is fringed with mangrove creeks, tidal sand flats, saltwater marsh, low coastal dunes and a coastal lagoon, at Buniadu Point, in the northern section. In the winter season the isle is often visited by dolphins.

The two main villages of Jinack Kajata and Jinack Niji, are in the north-eastern end of the largely sandy isle, while the international boundary between Gambia and Senegal runs through the northern end of the isle. However, the local Mandinka and Serer inhabitants move freely across the border to Djinack Diatako, a fishing orientated village across the border, in the Saloum Delta National Park.

Accommodation:
There are a few holiday accommodation choices on the resort isle's coastal fringes. There is the long established eco-retreat, located on the beach, called Madiyana Safari Lodge, which has 8 Gambian styled round huts, each sleeping 2 guests. The bathing facilities are shared and there is a bar and restaurant on site, but no generator. The other place to stay on the seafront is Jinack Lodge, an eco-lodge with solar power, located on an almost deserted beachfront, facing the Atlantic Ocean. It has 4 double and single

bedroom huts, each with an ensuite shower, wash-hand basin and toilet. The lodge also has a full restaurant and bar service, and has set up a few hammocks on the beach. They have no generator but have solar power instead to run all the basics.

Beach Area:
The beaches on Jinack Island are not what you would compare to say the Caribbean; the waters are shallow at low tide, but not turquoise blue; and because of coastal erosion sea waves lap the palm trees, Tamarix and other scrub at high tide. At low tide the beach is broad and flat with a slight slope, making the golden-gray sand ideal for strolling or checking out various objects the ocean has brought up such as sea shells and jellyfish. The occasional cow, sheep or villager will often wonder by. Because the sea water is generally shallow at low tide it is good for swimming.

Tourist Attractions & Things to Do:

Bird Watching
Jinack Island has a respectable range of bird habitats in a compact land area and is a superb site for bird watching enthusiasts. The habitats include mangrove swamps, mudflats, dry woodland, salt marsh, grassland, lagoons, dunes and beach flats. The shallow waters just after the north shore provide

superb feeding grounds for gulls, terns, and other piscivorous species which roost in significant numbers off Buniadu Point, on the northernmost shore and its coastal lagoon. The area is frequented by European migratory birds wintering here.

Among some of the bird species recorded here are Great Egrets, Storm-petrels, Slender-billed Gulls, Goliath Herons, Ospreys, Abyssinian Rollers, Royal Terns, Purple Herons, Senegal Parrots, Slender-billed Gulls, Red-billed Hornbills, Royal Terns, Beautiful Sunbirds, European Spoonbills, Yellow-backed Weavers, Greater Flamingos, Pelicans, Rose-ringed Parakeets, Laughing Doves, Greater Blue-eared Glossy Starlings, Northern Red Bishops (f), Green Wood-hoopoes, Senegal Thick-knees and Little Bee-eaters.

Boat Cruises
These can sometimes be arranged with your ground tour operator however, you can go to Denton Bridge and hire a boat to take you on a day trip. Some of the fishing ground tour operators will already have tailor-made packages that includes Jinack. While there it is easy to rent an African pirogue (narrow canoe) with rower, to take you around the various bolongs (creeks) and between the mangroves. Beware that most don't supply life jackets so this kind of trip is not for non-swimmers.

Dolphin Spotting

Mostly between December and January schools of bottlenose dolphins can often be seen swimming off the coast or even escorting your boat. Less conspicuous off the coast are the Atlantic Humpbacked Dolphins (Sousa teuszii).

Eating & Drinking

There are a number of beach bars along the beachfront of Jinack Island. You can also readily visit bars and restaurants in the various lodges. Consider also the place known as the Kayira Beach Resort. where they serve African dishes, BBQs on the beach along with a selection of soft and alcoholic drinks. There is also the Camara Sambou Beach Bar - Tel no: 7789295.

Nature Treks & Wildlife Spotting

There are lots of paths around Jinack Island, so just take along appropriate equipment and clothing. You might be lucky to spot various monitor lizards, mongoose, vervet monkeys, bushbuck, wildcats and even snakes! However, most species of snake in Gambia aren't poisonous, but be alert.

Sports Fishing

With good rod and tackle there are a number of fish species you can catch within the mangrove creeks by canoe as well as offshore deep sea fishing in the

Atlantic Ocean. Among some of the fish species are Red Snapper, Shads, African Threadfin and Mullet. To arrange a trip you would need to visit Denton Bridge, in Banjul, and arrange for a day trip to cruise and explore the mangrove creeks or using a more modern power boat to fish off the Jinack coast.

Visit the Local Villages by Donkey Cart

Because there are no taxis on the island, and only a few tour operator owned vehicles, one of the few forms of transport is by donkey powered cart. This is often an enjoyable and unique experience, moving slowly through rural paths, taking in the sights and sounds of nature at a leisurely pace. You can of course also walk to the villages of Niji and Kajata, and see how local people live, and maybe visit the local school.

Visit Senegal

The easiest way to go to Senegal is to get to the northern most part of the island which has the international boundary cutting across it. Villagers move between the boarder with impunity, however, as a tourist you should beware of your visitor status and holiday insurance conditions, lest something unexpected occurs. The safer option is to arrange this with Jinack Lodge who organise day-trip excursions into the Fathala Wildlife Reserve in Senegalese, which is approximately 6,000 hectares of protected forest park. You can also spend the day sampling restaurants, tourist craft markets and experiencing a little Franco-African culture.

Health & Safety:
It is fairly safe during the day. In the evening do not venture beyond the immediate vicinity of your lodgings alone at night, and have a few torches handy.

Though there are numerous cannabis farms here it is still illegal in Gambia. Don't be tempted.

TRAVEL INFORMATION & HOW TO GET THERE:

To get to Jinack Island you hop onto a boat ferry from the Banjul ports area to Barra. From Barra you then take a taxi heading towards Fass, then go left at Kanuma into the nature park. There are a couple of villages in the area: Kajata and Niji. It is possible to make a day-trip there from Kololi resort if you set out fairly early in the morning. The most convenient and easiest way is to go by power boat which can be hired at Denton Bridge in Banjul's Oyster Creek.

! When coming to the resort you need to know what to pack. There are no supermarkets and stores around and all the 'modern' conveniences are provided by your lodgings within the area.

! Other common spelling variations of the island are: Jinnak, Ginack or Jenack.

Travel to Kartong

Introduction:
Kartong Village and Kartong beach ecotourism resort are located in Kombo South District, in the West Coast Region on the southern tip of the southwest coast of The Gambia, in West Africa. The rural settlement lies on the Kombo Coastal Road, near its termination, and near the international border with the Senegal, which is demarcated by the Allahein River (San Pedro River). Kartong (also spelt Kartung) is a multi-ethnic village community, largely made up of Mandinka, followed by Jola, and other minority tribes such as Karoninka and Balanta. The village has a population of about 5,500 people; is about 60km from Banjul capital, and is one of the smallest and oldest settlements in Kombo South.

Accommodation:
There are a handful of basic to luxury lodges and camps along the coast, as well as inland. There is a decent guesthouse in the town itself and is part of the Lemonfish Art Gallery. It has 5 guestrooms with modern facilities and breakfast. If you want a room

on the waterfront then see the Boboi Beach Lodge with its shared bathing facilities, 12 round huts, a bar and restaurant and you can pitch your tent there too. Another place to stay is the Halahin Lodge, which is on the seafront and has 5 African style round huts and a restaurant. There is also the luxury Sandele Bay Eco Retreat.

Beach Area:

This far south on the Atlantic Ocean coast you can find some of The Gambia's most deserted, wild and picturesque bays, where the dry sand feels softer with a cleaner, more consistent colour than in any of the other resorts beaches along the 10.5km strip of coastline. As you move further south along the Kartong promontory, the palm tree fringed beaches seems to get a little wider and there is an access route leading directly from the northern end of the village to the beachfront. Occasionally you will see fishermen from nearby Gunjur, as well as Senegal and Ghana pull in shad, sharks and squid for the fishmongers to trade from the shed that makes up the fish market in this secluded corner. Various animals such as herds of cows will occasionally make an appearance - they are usually fairly docile though, so they shouldn't disturb your sunbathing.

The beachfront is also a superb location for camping, but do ask for advice from the Kartung Association for Responsible Tourism (KART), who have a Visitor Centre information office in the centre of town. (Tel no: 4495887)

General Area:

The main built-up settlement is encircled by ocean, scrub, dune swales, and to the east, streams, desolate salt pans and mangrove swamps which are adjacent to the River Allahein (also known as the Halahin or Hallahin Bolong). The main Kombo Coastal Road cuts through the settlement and ends a few kilometres further south at the banks of the river.

Founding Family History:

According to oral history, Kartong village was founded by the (Buwaro) Buwarow family, who migrated from Guinea Bissau to Gambia over 450 years ago. They were later joined by the Sonko, Touray, Manneh, Jabang and Jammeh families respectively. The most obvious reason for the settlement's location was to gain easy access the sea and river for fishing.

Tourist Attractions & Things to Do:

Folonko Crocodile Pool

Also known as the Mama Folonko Sacred Shrine and Museum, the crocodile pool is located about 200 meters away from the highway on the South West of the Kartong village and is claimed to have been founded by the leader of the Tijaniyya sect in West Africa, Sheikh Umar Futiu Taal, in the first half of 19th century.

Folonko, one of The Gambia's three sacred sites with crocodiles pools, is about 1.12 hectares in size, and the pond in the centre has a 10 meter radius and is enclosed by gallery forest. The site is under the auspices of the National Centre for Arts & Culture in Banjul.

Replenished by a source of freshwater and covered in a layer of pakanju-water lettuce, the pool is located in a shaded grove of kobo figs and rhun palms. The place is more remote and visited by far fewer tourists than its counterpart at Kachikally in Bakau. It is used as a place of pilgrimage where people bring gifts in return for good fortune, at a time of crisis or to help women overcome infertility. Older women from two of Kartong's groups, Christian Karoninka Mandinkas and Muslim Mandinka visit to pray and request for help a few times a week. They also oversee visitors, who come here with offers of cash, Kola nuts, grain salt or other gifts.

Gambia Reptiles Farm

Going southbound the reptile centre is located just before you get to the village. The place is really a conservation area where you can see various reptiles up close such as snakes, (both venomous and non-venomous), including Nile monitor lizards, Agama lizards, turtles, crocodiles, Senegalese chameleons, geckos, spitting cobras, as well as non-reptiles such as centipedes. The Gambia Reptiles Farm also tries to educate local people about the benefits of having snakes in their local environment, for example in keeping the mice and rat population under control. The entry fee is about £2.50 (Tel no: +220 779 5008 email: paziaud@yahoo.fr).

Bird Watching
More than 260 bird species have been recorded at Kartong in varying habitats which are tidal mud flats, mangrove swamps, sand dunes, Guinea savannah scrubland, foreshore, remnant of high forest and rice paddies. Parts of the area used to be excavated for sand for the building industry. This activity has long been halted and the old sand pits now fill up with water from the rainy season and as a result is now a magnet for numerous indigenous and Palaearctic migratory birds.

Among species you can expect to see here are the Malachite Kingfisher, African jacana and crake, European Roller, Pygmy Goose, Green Sandpiper,

Peregrine Falcon, Wryneck, African Collared Dove, Woodchat Shrike, Marsh Sandpiper, Painted Snipe, Purple Swamphen, Blue-naped Mouse Bird, and many others.

You can also visit the Kartong Bird Observatory which is on the edge of a disused sand mine. The research station rings and studies birds in its central wetlands recording area. KBO also has trained bird guides, refreshments and accommodation can be arranged. They even have courses on Senegambian cooking, as well as organising bush walks.

Sports Fishing
Stala Adventures is a fishing and birding resort who are based in the area, and even provide basic but clean accommodation located on the river bank. The kinds of fish species you can expect to catch are red snapper, barracuda, catfish and puffer fish.

Kartong Festival
The village hosts the yearly festival which offers visitors an opportunity to experience local culture and traditions in the form of music, art and dance from The Gambia, Senegal and other West African countries. The inaugural event was hosted in November 2005 and is now held once a year in February. The festival usually starts with a traditional procession through the streets, and

performances in nearby lodges and other venues, ending at the arena, for an evening of traditional and modern dance, music and mask parades. (Tel no: 9933193)

Lemonfish Art Gallery

This is a privately operated fine African art gallery, film-house and guest house rolled into one. The Lemonfish Art Gallery hosts exhibitions on contemporary African painting, sculptures and other pieces produced by Gambians and other artists in West Africa. They also show African films and offer courses in pottery and batik making.

Kartong Association For Responsible Tourism

The KART Visitor Centre is your first port of call if you intend to get the most out of the village and surrounding locality. They can provide you with travel information, local guides for birdwatching, fishing, dug-out canoe cruises around the mangroves or bush trekking, and you can even hire bicycles to more easily explore the rural location.

The main goal of KART is to promote the resort as an ecotourist holiday destination, and try to avoid some of the negative impacts of tourism on the local environment. Money that is generated by their activities goes towards improving local amenities in the settlement and helping local villagers.

River Allahein

This is the southern end of the Gambian coastline which terminates at the mouth of the Allahein River. A series of dynamic sand spits and beach ridges runs parallel to the shore from 'Kartong Point' to the mouth of the river. You might want to take a pirogue cruise to explore the saltwater creeks and mangroves on your side of the river border. There are plenty of fishermen willing to take you for a fee of course.

If you go by bike from the village, you can ride further south along the main road to the most southern end of the west coast. After the military checkpoint you go south a short way where you will come face to face with the Allahein River, where the road turns right towards the beach's small fishing centre. If you turn left you will get to the fish houses. Straight ahead of you is the estuary and beyond is the Casamance region in Senegal. It is possible to cross the water from Kartong and visit Kabadio, Diannah, Abene and Kafountine, but you must get an exit stamp on your passport first. Please note that this area of Senegal has seen separatist unrest in the past; therefore you should seek advice on traveling there from your own country first.

Restaurants and Bars

There is an Italian restaurant called Vincenza's pizzeria (formerly Franco's) at the end of the road on the left fork, just after the fish smoking houses. It is situated on the river bank and gives you beautiful, unspoilt views of the saltwater mangroves on the other side in Casamance.

Health & Safety:
Being close to the border crossing the town is fairly safe having a good military presence there as well as a police station. Be careful about venturing out alone on foot at night outside the settlement or you lodgings, and do carry a pocket torchlight after sunset, even in your accommodation as lights can suddenly go out.

Also avoid swimming in the Allahein River or near its estuary as the tidal currents can be strong.

Travel Information:
To get to Kartong from Gambia's Banjul Airport just take a green taxi which will take you south via the district capital of Brikama town, and down towards the south west coast. When travelling to the village please note that this is as far south as you can go by car as the Kombo Coastal Road terminates at the estuary of the Allahein River. You will find a military checkpoint just after the centre of the village on the main road.

If you are thinking of going into Casamance in Senegal then do seek official advice from your country.

If you are intending on staying here for more than a few days then do take along enough personal supplies such as toiletries. If you do run out then you can re-fill by going to the nearest area with a sufficient number of shops is Gunjur, and there is a small mini-market inside the Elton Petrol Station in Tanji.

Travel to Kololi

Introduction:

The Kololi resort town and Senegambia Strip tourist area began life as a typical coastal fishing village, set back from the Atlantic Ocean, in the Kombo St. Mary District, Western Region of The Gambia, West Africa. The village is 18km from the Banjul capital. Since the early 1980s Kololi has been radically transformed by tourism, growing significantly and spreading right down to the beach, at what are now called the Palma Rima and Senegambia resort areas. Since the completion of the GamNor or Gambia-Norway Hotel in 1982 (now known as the Senegambia Beach Hotel), as well as the establishment of the tourist craft market in the same year, the town has seen a massive growth in the accommodation sector, and other tourism related industries. The original settlement, Kololi Village, is now home to an increasing number of professionals, expats, retirees and workers in the hospitality industry.

Accommodation:

Depending on your preferences there are numerous types of holiday accommodation dotted around Kololi. From tourist-class hotels, to guesthouses, lodges, B&Bs and self-catering accommodation. Standards and room costs can vary widely, from a simple budget priced room in a down-at-heel guesthouse, to a luxury hotel suite with air conditioning and an ensuite bathroom.

Tourist Attractions & Things To Do:

Craft Market

One of the area's biggest draws is the purpose built, lively Senegambia Craft Market (a bengdula), which was first built in 1982, re-built in 1990 and subsequently re-built again on the junction in 2001, with a capacity of about 64 stalls. It has a respectable choice of locally made souvenir handicrafts, including carved wooden masks and djembe drums, basketware, paintings of landscapes, people, wildlife, tie and dye, jewellery, beaded necklaces, leather handbags, sandals, shoes, colourful batik wraps, and food such as cakes, hot sauce and dark honey, fresh from local women's co-operatives. The stallholders are bound by an agreed code of conduct, which prohibits hassling visitors for their custom. Those who breach the code are liable to suspension for a fixed term.

Mandela's Seafood and Steak House Restaurant

Kololi Village

On the other side of the Bertil Harding Highway from the tourist strip, is a calmer, more peaceful residential district of sandy roads and family homes. There is a relatively new paved road from the Senegambia Junction connecting to Kololi Road and onwards to the old village and Manjai Kunda. This route has already begun to rapidly develop with restaurants, bars and other tourist amenities. Around this area is a smattering of basic facility guesthouses, and several venues to learn dance, music and painting. There is the 'Village Gallery' Bar & Restaurant which is a privately run art gallery which exhibits and sells paintings, sculptures, and photographs for West African and Gambian artists. It also organises art workshops / lectures for individuals and institutions, arranges art and cultural trips through local tour operators, uses their contacts to arrange for cultural and musical performances and above all encourages its partners to work in a way that preserves the social and cultural heritage of The Gambia. Special lectures are also organised as it is intended to be also used as a focal point for aspiring and established local handicraft professionals. (Tel no: 4463646 or 9917343)

The Beach Area

In late 2003 the Kololi resort beaches were replenished (nourished), by a Dutch company called Delft Hydraulics, with about 1 million cubic meters of sand over 1.5km of its length, with a width of 120 meters. This was done to reverse previous coastal erosion that had seriously compromised the resort area's ability to continue to attract large numbers of foreign tourists.

When sunbathing put on some good sunscreen with a high SPF as there are usually few clouds in the sky during the winter season and the mid-day sun can be unrelenting. The day-time temperatures are simply too much for sunbathers to lie out in the open sand for extended periods of time. This is where the beach bar's huts provide much needed respite with their thatched, woven palm roofs and canopies.

Kololi's beach bars are a vivid and quintessential part of the Atlantic Ocean's scenery and provides a more relaxing, scenic alternative to their inland counterparts. They often play reggae on their portable sound systems, and the occasional visit by dance troupes or local singers to liven up things a little in the evenings. These are convenient places to chat with some of the locals. Food here is usually cheaper, typically comprised of shrimps or fish, oven baked in silver foil such as red snapper, ladyfish and barracuda, with a small choice of drinks. Fresh fruit pressers' stalls also dot the coastline and are inspected and regulated by the Tourism Board to ensure they conform to minimum set hygiene standards.

The Village Complex

Also known as the Horseshoe Shopping Complex this is as close as you can get to a European style shopping mall. It is a unique, modern building on two floors, and the shaped like half a doughnut, located on the Bertil Harding Highway, opposite the Total Petrol Station. Is has a supermarket, clothes stores, a fountain, cafes selling cakes, drinks and ice cream, varied restaurants, some offices, a nice central garden, a rooftop terrace accessed by two spiral staircases, car parking space, and a children's playground, to keep the kids occupied while you shop or dine. The Village Complex is a landmark you can easily spend all afternoon at, and there are no shortages of taxis to take you back to your hotel or guest house.

Quad Biking

This method of getting around, and exploring the locality and beyond, is growing in popularity. You can hire a quad bikes from near the junction at 'Freedom Hire' near the Binis Bar and the Britannia Pub. Sometimes all-terrain vehicles (ATVs) are available directly on the beachfront.

Quad bikeWest African Powersports offers guided quad biking safaris as well as buggies along dirt roads to Tujering. They can pick you up and drop you off by car at any of the hotels in the main resorts such as Kololi or Kotu and take you to the start of the safari which is at Brusubi and goes to Tujering beach for lunch. From there it's back to Brusubi and a drop-off at your accommodation.

Tilly's Tours, on the Senegambia Strip, also offers quad bike safaris (Tel no: 9800215 or 7707356). Note: before getting on one of these do make sure that quad biking is covered by your travel insurance policy.

Restaurants

Kololi, and in particular the Senegambia vicinity, has a profusion of different restaurants scattered throughout, especially along the main tourist thoroughfare and nearby roads, serving a broad range of international cuisine. There are various types of restaurants serving Indian, Italian, Thai, Chinese, Lebanese and European food on their menus. Near the corner from the craft market is Gaya Art Cafe & Restaurant, a unique diner which displays and sells art and craft artifacts from around the world. They also serve top quality, international cuisine and drinks in a shaded, relaxed small garden setting at the front. If you want to try some authentic Gambian food then you are best advised to go deeper into the district, in some of the private local restaurants or along the easterly road from Palma Rima, heading away from the beach.

The village also has a diverse mix of restaurants, bars and clubs, tempting to people wishing for a change from the mass-tourism feel of Kololi's mainstream diners and nightspots, as well as independent travellers. As you travel further south towards Kerr Serign the options of restaurants are more limited, but growing each year along the coast and in the nearby residential neighbourhoods.

Night Clubs

Whether you like your nightclubs small and cosy or large and spectacular there is something for you. Near the Senegambia Strip is the Aquarius, plush, compact, within easy walking distance of Sarges Hotel, and playing pop and hip hop mixes till late. There is also the Club Paparazzi which is right on the strip, again small, nice bar and a tiny, central dance floor. The 'Wow' is also nearby; a bit rough and frequented mostly by locals, but has reasonably priced drinks and seating area outside. If you want something resembling a large, dedicated nightclub then you can't do better that the massive Duplex Nightclub. It is a huge complex with several bars, a large, purpose built dance floor, numerous automated disco lights, a high ceiling and a thumping, pumping sound system.

Dream Park

It opened in Kololi in 2008 at a cost of over $2 million; this is Gambia's first dedicated amusement park and well worth visiting. Dream Park Entertainment Centre is located on the Bertil Harding Highway, near the road leading to the Sunswing Hotel on the beach side area. The theme park is crammed full of rides for all the family such as a spacecraft, bumper cars, battle castle for kids, Tilt-A-Whirl, a crescent swing, bumper boat, and the happy express. It plays host to small musical concerts and other similar events. There is also a modern restaurant, a toy and sweet shop and toilet facilities. Please note that it is not advisable to leave children unaccompanied within the grounds.

Bijilo Forest Park

Also known as Monkey Park; the nature trail can be reached by walking south from Sarges Hotel, near the tourist strip, for about 500m and you will see the wire fence and trees of Bijilo Forest Park in front of you. To get in however, you turn right and walk down for about 100 metres and the entrance is to your left, clearly marked by a ticket office. Monkey Park covers an area of about 0.5 sq. km of beach side woodland reserve. The reserve is dominated by proud rhun palms which once flourished along the coastline of The Gambia. The vegetation also includes tall deciduous trees, shrubs, and savanna grassland. The forest floor has plants such as vines, lilies, wild orchids, cotton trees. Once inside there is a very good chance of spotting vervet monkey, red colobus, a few squirrels and a plethora of birds.

Bird Watching

Kololi's beach hotel area is not the best birdwatching territory, but there are still opportunities to see over 70 species for the amateur and professional who wants to stay near or in their hotel. There is the Bijilo Forest Park which is within easy walking distance from the tourist strip. The closed forest and coastal scrub is home to over 130 species such as the Palm-nut Vulture, White-throated Bee-eater, Peregrine Falcon, Little Bee-eater, Stone Partridge and the Ahanta Francolin. Some of the larger hotels themselves are good bird spotting grounds due to their plentiful vegetation of palms, trees, bushes and shrubs. They actually have a policy of encouraging avian visitors through specially created bird gardens.

Among the species of birds visiting the Senegambia and Kairaba hotels you might see poking in out out of the hibiscus variable sunbirds, with their small, delicately curved beaks and colourful plumage. You might also see cattle egrets, red cheeked cordon-bleu, Abyssinian roller, brown and red-billed firefinch, Caspian terns, yellow-crowned gonolek (shrike), Senegalese coucals, starlings, chestnut-crowned sparrow weaver and many more of our feathered friends.

Horse Riding
If you like to do a bit of horseback riding on Kololi's strand, then ask at your reception desk. They should know a few operators nearby. You can also contact Lama Bony who arranges horse riding along the northern Kombo beachfront.

Women's Skills Centre:

The training project was the idea of two German visitors who founded it in 1997, and its aims are to help young women from the Kololi village gain skills in sewing and design, batik and tie dye, embroidery and other handicrafts, as well as teaching them to write and speak some basic English.

Palma Rima Area:

The Palma Rima resort is comprised of a relatively small group of hotels (dominated by the Bakadaji Hotel, Palma Rima Hotel and its crossroads), lodges, restaurants and small clubs located between 150m southeast of the Bertil Harding Highway (aka Kombo Coastal Road) and the Atlantic Ocean's beach, about 1km southwest of bridge at Kotu Stream. On one side of the junction are fruit and vegetable, and fish sellers' stalls. Though obviously touristic in appearance, it's relatively modest in contrast to the main tourist hotspot, 1.5km further to the southwest. If you are looking for a good quality self-catering accommodation near the beach with a pool then try Luigi's Holiday Apartments (which also has a great Italian restaurant). If you're looking for a night spot / bar and diner then try Shiraz Restaurant. Further towards the beachfront is the popular Solomon's Beach Bar & Restaurant, right on the sand and facing the ocean, serving good food and drinks. For more budget priced places you need to go further inland, but try and stay within 200m or so from the main coastal road.

Senegambia Area:

The Senegambia Strip - Kololi's central beach resort, named after the country's biggest hotel, is the hub of The Gambia's tourist activity, with a bustling, mostly fairly tacky strip of bars, restaurants, and nightclubs, and a variety of tourist-class hotels. This is strictly not a residential location; the area is designated in the Tourism Development Area (TDA) and is meant only for visitors. At times it is one of the most bumster-riddled locations on the coast; until the local paramilitary police clamp down do their numbers suddenly melt away. Development in the adjacent area, particularly on the main highway, is proceeding at a frenetic pace, and the results are not always pleasing. You will often come across tacky plaster sculptures of people and animals placed outside diners and bars and bizarre mouldings fixed on building façades. Along the strip are restaurants, bars and clubs galore as well as several bureaus de change, the Standard Chartered Bank, a few mini-markets, a net cafe, souvenir shops, car hire, green tourist taxis etc.

Health & Safety:

After endless decades of darkness along the coastal highway, street lighting was installed in 2006, which starts at the main traffic lights in Fajara and goes all the way south to the airport, as well as Brufut, and other locations, thereby increasing safety for tourists who venture out on foot at night. The sides of the roads have had extra gravel added to provide more of a 'walkway', reducing your chances of getting hit by a vehicle. Watch your back though as bikes also use it, as well as taxis pulling over for passengers. It's best to walk towards the traffic.

If you are going out at night do carry your money in a money belt, and carry a small torchlight. Crime, such as muggings, are pretty low, but it pays to be vigilant. Avoid unfamiliar places at night and try to walk with a companion. Try and get a sim card from one of the mobile phone operators and keep some useful numbers handy, like the hotel reception, a taxi driver known to you, a friend and so on. It does no harm to tell someone where you are going, day or night. Finally, note that the nearest fire station is in Kotu.

Travel Information:

To get to Kololi village from Gambia's Banjul Airport you taxi hire or car hire and drive north, until the Brusubi Roundabout, then continue straight north along the Kombo Coastal Road, and past Bijilo, for a further 4 km. The cost of taxi rides is posted just outside the entrance to the airport, usually on your right side at the exit. It should cost you less than £10.

To travel out-and-about there are green tourist taxis outside the major hotels, but they do cost more than the yellow taxis which can be found on the highway outside of the Senegambia Strip, about 150m from the junction on your left.

Travel to Kotu

Introduction:

Kombo Beach HotelThe Kotu resort and village in Gambia is in the Kombo Saint Mary District, in the West Coast Region, and forms one half of the main centre of Gambia's coastal tourist industry, with the other being in Kololi. The village is 17km from the Banjul capital. The Badala Highway leads from the Bertil Harding Highway and crosses the creek (aka River Sando or Sandu) at the bridge and proceeds to Kotu Strand. Partly enclosing the beach based tourist enclave is the Kotu Stream, rice fields and the Fajara Golf Course behind. The focal point of the area is the BB Craft Market (Bengdula), an oval, half enclosure, lined with souvenir shops, bars, restaurants and other amenities. Just outside the market entrance are bureau de change, minimarkets, taxis and other hospitality services.

Accommodation:

In the Kotu holiday resort, the accommodation choices are all medium or large tourist-class hotels, mostly supported or owned by some of the big tour operators, either on, or very near to respectable length of beach. They are mostly low-rise and blend in well with the scenery. The Palm Beach and Sunset Beach hotels are nestled close to the stream and face the Atlantic Ocean, while the Kombo Beach Hotel and the Bungalow Beach Hotel are a little to the north east and are also on the strand. The Bakotu Hotel lies on the opposite side of the craft market and has no beachfront.

Beach Area:

The coconut palm fringed Kotu beach area has a reasonably good width to the waters edge and the sand is of good quality however, the sea water is sandy. Around the Palm Beach Hotel are some small lagoons with far less turbulent water. This section of the Atlantic Ocean ranges from flat calm to choppy with the occasional small waves lapping at the shore. It's shallow enough to allow you to get out to a reasonable distance from the shore (about 25 metres), but then the shelf drops steeply, so do be alert. Often there are waves breaking up to 300m off-shore. You sometimes see numerous chaotic waves building fast, with a flat shore break to surf. There are lifeguards based on the beach with their own high lookout post. Be aware of the warning flags they put out to warn about current swimming conditions.

General Area:

Palm Beach HotelAs your flight comes over the Kotu Point area en-route to Yundum's Banjul International Airport you'll see the Gambia's coastline with good number of hotel swimming pools scattered among the palm trees, rice paddy fields and sandy roads. You won't however see any residential houses, except inland, behind the coastal road to your left. On this coastal strip called the TDA, the tourist infrastructure takes precedence. During the five months of the low-season, when many of the hotels, restaurants and bars are closed, the locality is quiet and sleepy, only gearing into life towards the end of the monsoon in late September / early October, when the restaurateurs, bar owners and hoteliers get on with their yearly repairs and repainting program. As soon as the first peak-season visitors arrive in mid-October, does it metamorphosize into a bustling, gregarious package-holiday resort once again.

The dirt path that meanders from the Badala Highway, past the connecting road to the Palm Beach Hotel, and on into Kololi resort, is a pleasurable 1.5 mile stroll. The Kotu Stream area is particularly beautiful during the rice-growing season (Aug-Nov), when the fields are an emerald green. By the end of the dry season, the creek is almost dry, but at any time of year there are many birds species and tall, mature palm trees to admire, and sometimes you might see vervet monkeys and monitor lizards. You'll often see plastic bottles clustered round the tops of the palms, and palm wine tappers shinning up to collect the fermenting sap. This area is also used by cattle herders so don't be surprised if you see cows making their way along the shoreline, as well as the roads and fields.

Tourist Attractions & Things to Do:

Craft Market

Also known as the BB Hotel Tourist Craft Market Bendula, it was established on the shore in 1975 to regulate the activities of Gambian women selling baskets to holidaymakers. It is an open-air, oval shaped courtyard with a central roundabout which is surrounded by approximately 42 souvenir shops, restaurants, and fruit sellers. It is also used as the main entrance to the strand by hotel guests, and lies between the Kombo Beach and Bungalow Beach hotels. Here you can find tourist souvenirs such as wooden masks, batik and tie dye clothing, African jewellery, oil and sand paintings, handmade leather shoes, bags, beachwear, kaftans, djembe drums and more. There are also bureau de change, mini-markets etc. From the entrance and to your left there are several bars and restaurants.

On Kotu's Atlantic Ocean beachfront end there are a number of fruit stalls offering freshly squeezed juices and whole fruits such as oranges, mangoes, papaya, bananas and other local tropical fruits. There are various fruit stalls spread out along the beachfront which are regulated by the Gambia Tourism Board, and the women are forbidden from pestering tourists for their business, though this doesn't stop them beckoning tourists for their trade however. These women can be identified by their green T-shirt uniforms.

Cycling

You can hire bicycles just outside most of the hotels on the strand. There is also a bicycling track which follows the northern fence of the Badala Hotel, and continues for a few hundred metres to the back of the Palma Rima Hotel in Kololi. It is possible to ride a bike at low tide all the way to Kololi, just make sure you have good, rugged tyres. Another possible nearby route is to cross the road and make your way to the road leading into the Kotu Power Station. Where it forks left it leads you eventually to Manjai's urban area and its main road. The area around the stations is relatively quiet with plenty of trees and scrubland.

Sunbathing

Sunbathing here is pretty straight forward but be aware you are exposed to the full glare of the sun on most days between November to April - clouds are few and far between at this time of the year. Try taking little breaks under you parasol every once in a while and use a good sun cream with high factor.

Horse Riding

There are a number of people operating horseback riding sessions along the strand. You can also enquire at your reception desk about any local operators near where you stay.

Harriet Horse Riding Stable

Restaurants

Kotu's lively holiday resort image is reflected in its density of touristy venues to eat and drink. In this vicinity there are also lots of juice bars, beach bars and fruit stands. You will find various kinds of restaurants, starting from strand itself all the way through the craft market and onto the Badala Highway, up to the Elton junction and beyond. Among these are:

a) Al Baba GFC

b) Boss Lady

c) Captain's Table

d) Garden Kitchen

e) Hong-Mei Chinese Restaurant

f) Jamaican Spice

g) JD's

h) John Raymond's Bar & Restaurant

i) Julas

j) Kunta Kinteh's Beach Bar

k) Ninke Nanka

l) Oscars

m) Paradise Beach Bar & Restaurant

n) Paradiso Pizza

o) Sailor's,

p) Samba's Kitchen

q) Tandoor

r) and many others.

s) Birdwatching

Kotu's tourist-class hotels are very near to a number of bird habitats, making this an ideal centre for birders visiting Gambia. The area is made up of mangroves, coastal scrub land and rice fields which provides a relatively easy introduction to West African birding. There is an abundance of bird species and populations here due to almost no human habitation here and the spacious areas of natural habitat with lots of water, bush and trees.

A good starting point for birdwatching professionals is the Fajara Golf Course where the short grass of the fairways is alluring to the likes of Senegal wattled plover, black-headed plover, piapiac and the long-tailed glossy starling. The areas of scrub and trees can yield up an amazing variety of birds. Some of the more regular species included red-billed hornbill, yellow-billed shrike, green wood-hoopoe, grey woodpecker, black-billed wood dove, black-cap babblers, beautiful sunbirds, double-spurred francolin, bronze manikin and bearded barbet.

From here you can walk across the golf course at Fajara, and you will come too Kotu Stream, a tidal creek bordered by rice paddies and mangrove wetlands. Several species of Palearctic waders are commonly found along the stream, along with Senegal thick-knee. Plenty of grey-headed gulls roost on the mud at low tide and various herons and egrets are easily spotted here. Around the area you can spot giant pied and malachite kingfishers and red-chested swallows. The Kotu Bridge is well known as a place to find Gambian trained bird guides for hire.

Another good area to go visit the sewage ponds, which can be accessed by a footpath on the other side of the road from the Badala Park; it is behind the Elton Petrol Station. At the sewage works the productive pond life here lures many bird species; you may see waders like wood and marsh sandpiper and spur-winged plovers, pink-backed pelicans, white-faced whistling ducks and white-winged black terns. Little swifts are regulars and the surrounding scrub had starlings and fork-tailed drongo.

Health & Safety:
Between the tourist village and about 250 meters before the well-lit section of road, is mostly wilderness and farmland. The road itself is lit along its entire length making it possible to walk at night. However, it is advisable to take a cab, if possible, to and from your hotel after 9pm. If you have to walk, then make sure you are with several other people and always carry a pocket torch light just in case.

The area around the Strand is fairly safe and there is a Gambian tourist police post there, as well as at the start of the road leading in from the Bertil Harding Highway. Not far from the junction of the highway, towards Manjai, is the fire station.

Travel Information:
There are green tourist taxis parked within the vicinity of the accommodations on Kotu Strand. Yellow taxis are only permitted to enter to drop off their passengers but not allowed to wait, unless they get special permission.

Travel to Makasutu

Introduction:
Makasutu Culture Forest is a private, ecotourism woodland reserve in the Kombo Central District, of the West Coast Region of The Gambia in West Africa. The woodland is 5 kilometres to the northeast of Brikama town, and is directly south of the Banjul capital. The nature park has a land area of 405 hectares (1,000 acres) and encompasses the Mandina Bolong, a tributary of the Gambia River. The protected wilderness is a pristine expanse of riverine, palm and hardwood-forest, mangrove creek, savanna and salt-flat ecosystems.

Accommodation:

Within the conservation area is the award winning, luxury eco-lodge called Mandina Lodges, the country's top holiday eco-resort, created by two Englishmen from London. It's said that during its construction no trees were felled in Makasutu Culture Forest, and the lodges were designed to fit available gaps between trees. Local people in neighbouring settlements, such as Kembujeh Village, were employed during construction, as hotel staff and as tour guides on the reserve.

Background & History:
Myths & Legends

Makasutu is a Mandinka word: 'Maka' is Islam's holy place of Mecca, and 'Sutu' means forest, which translates to 'holy forest'. The original name 'Maka Sutu' dates back to the 12th century when Islam swept down into the Senegambia region from the Sahara. Mandinka folklore, traced back to the 12th century, says that a dragon like creature lives in the swamp, known as the 'Ninki Nanka' (also known as Ninkinanka or Ninkinanko), and guards the buried clothes and crown of Mansa Jatta, a tribal king from the Soninke Kingdom of Busumbala, who was slain in battle by Kombo Sillah, a Muslim king. The Ninki Nanka is also believed to protect the woods, and adjacent community held orchards from potential thieves. Local legend also maintained that the woodland was haunted by spirits or 'djinns', as well as giants, and as a result, the sacred woodland was uninhabited, and used mostly for prayer and tribal rituals, such as the bathing of newly circumcised boys in the waters of the Mandina Bolong. Local kings forbade any hunting and tree felling on these sacred grounds.

As the 20th century progressed, migrants from Guinea settled in the area, with the permission of local kings, and began cultivating rice in the western section of Makasutu. With this encroachment people's fears of the 'Big Forest' began to diminish, and the area soon became a valuable source of wild food and timber for locals living in and around the vicinity.

Modern Day Development

The forest was on the brink of being cleared bare when in December 1992, two adventurous Britons, James English, an engineer, and Lawrence Williams, an architect, came to The Gambia to continue their 3 year search for a location to build an eco-retreat in the wilderness, and finally decided on a parcel of land in the Makasutu. Initially, local people and the Alkalo were reluctant to sell it to them based on the areas sacredness. Eventually they managed to acquire 4 acres of land from the Sanneh Kunda (family) who held ancient title to the land. The entrepreneurs' intention was to create a small camp oasis for adventure travellers and backpackers. After buying the land they departed to Europe on a 3 month trip. During their absence about 200 trees bordering the fence was cut down, and accelerated tree felling was underway, the spot's sanctity having been further eroded. With all of the deforestation that was occurring in the area, Sanneh Kunda, as well as the Department of Forestry, urged James and Lawrence to purchase the area to protect it.

Baboons Base camp

The initial plan for just a small base camp for backpackers was abandoned, and they eventually bought the remaining 4 square kilometres of land and proceeded to fence it. Over the next few years 15,000 trees were replanted, and 70 water wells were dug to keep them watered. The fenced area was now to be a nature and cultural reserve, emphasising how the local people live, and also to encourage the return of wildlife to the sub-tropical woodland and riverine. The local people that were living and utilizing the woods and streams, prior to the arrival of James and Lawrence, were permitted to stay on the land, meetings were held with them, and it was decided to integrate them into the sustainable eco-tourism venture that was in the pipeline. It took seven years to complete the project and the first place to be developed was called the 'Base Camp', followed by the Baobab Cultural Centre. Finally, on the 20th July 1999, Makasutu Culture Forest was open to tourists as well as the general Gambian public.

Many visitors expressed their wish to be able to sleep on the site because of the serenity they experienced at the ecological project. As a result of this feedback it was decided to further develop the site to include a 5 star, creekside eco-lodge, known as 'Mandina River & Jungle Lodges'. It incorporates sustainable measures, such as composting toilets, and solar-powered water heating and lighting systems. Designed by Lawrence, building began in 2000, and since its completion and opening in late 2002, the project has created alternative livelihoods in the community through the employment of over 250 local people from the nearby villages; and it is estimated that the wilderness project and Mandina River Lodges, indirectly benefits about 3,500 local people.

At Makasutu's Base Camp, an impressively tall, white viewing tower was opened in December 2013, straddled by two spiral staircases and 3 elevated viewing platforms. From here you can take in fantastic vistas of the palm trees, mangrove creeks, the Mandina Bolong and savanna habitats. You also get the chance to cool off in the irregular shaped swimming pool with its own island, set in a landscaped garden and dotted with palm trees and night lights. Visitors can also do a little shopping at the Craft Centre, where you can pick up wooden masks, drums and other tourist souvenirs. You can also see people weaving, silversmiths at work and other craftsmen. You can also try your hand at pottery, cooking, furniture making and a wood carving lesson.

Awards:

Mandina LodgesSince the opening of Makasutu and Mandina Lodges, the project has gone on to win several international awards, such as being voted the 'Best New Eco Hotel in The World' by the UK's Sunday Times (2003); 'Best Overseas Development' by the 'British Guild of Travel Writers Award' (2004); and has been highly commended at the 'Responsible Tourism Awards' as the 'Best Poverty Alleviation'. It has also featured in past editions of Travel Africa Magazine.

Nature Trail & Culture Tour:

Most tourist visitors come on the one-day organised excursion, including return transport to the resorts. The entry fee includes the standard full-day guided tour, including entertainment and lunch. However, your group size could number up to a couple of dozen. Independent travellers can choose to go on a full-day or half-day guided cultural / eco-tour. To get the most out of the full-day excursion to Makasutu Culture Forest, an early start is required. If the drive is from hotels in the main coastal resorts of Kololi, Kotu or Bijilo, then it takes about 1 hour to the nature park. If you are part of a ground tour operator organised day-trip, then on your arrival you begin by walking through woodland to the assembly area. From there your tour group then takes a nice stroll to the Baobab Bar and Restaurant, where you will be greeted and given a brief history of the place. On the way there you will see some tree stumps carved into sculptors, these are the remnants from the time locals were chopping down trees.

From here your itinerary can involve cruises along the mangrove creeks or guided foot treks. Along the nature trail through diverse ecosystems including Guinea savannah and tropical gallery woodland, your appointed guide might point to the various tree species, such as mahogany, rhun palms and baobab. Depending on the time of day you might see some birds and monkeys, though the simians here are more withdrawn than their counterparts in Bijilo. During your walk look out for the ubiquitous termite mounds, some over 2 metres high.

While along the bush walk you are likely to walk by the hut of a traditional Gambian medicine man, who produces and sells herbal potions of traditional medicines and remedies from trees and bushes growing in the area, as well as charms. The holy man or Marabout also reads palms and 'predicts' your future. Further on the trail you will get an opportunity to watch how a palm wine tapper hauls himself up a tree using a leather belt (traditionally a palm frond sling) which straps him loosely to the tree, to collect the sweet flower sap. You will also get the opportunity to sample some of the fermented wine.

Probably the best part of the day in Makasutu Culture Forest is the canoeing along the Mandina Bolong and adjacent mangrove creeks in an African pirogue, a wooden dugout canoe made from a single log of mahogany. This is a most relaxing cruise with some wonderful, close up views of the region's mangrove and palm fringed habitats. The meandering waters are calm and glistening, with lots of silence and serenity, and all you will hear as you drift down the waters are the sporadic bird calls, the constant dipping of the rower's paddle and the occasional chatter of the other tourists. You might spot Mangrove Sunbirds feeding off nectar, and African Darters swimming with only their head and neck above water while hunting for fish, or Lily Trotters walking on the floating vegetation of the mangrove swamp. Occasionally you will see local village fishermen at work or women collecting oysters from underwater roots. You might even be able to take a canoe ride to nearby Kubuneh Village, where you can visit the living art project called "Wide Open Walls". The idea is to paint some of the compounds in the Ballabu area with murals, and promote The Gambia as a desirable tourist destination. Note: if you bring along your own rod and tackle it is possible to try your hand at a little fishing from the main jetty on the Mandina Bolong.

There is an alfresco buffet lunch of organic Gambian food such as rice with peanut stew (Domoda), Jollof Rice with fish and vegetables, served back at the Baobab Restaurant, with its tall, spacious Bantaba (thatched, shaded structure).

After lunch comes the entertainment. A group of Makasutu based Jola dancers and drummers from the nearby Kembujeh Village, start their routine performance on a natural stage, under the gaze of a huge baobab tree. You are often encouraged to join in the dance. This however is not necessarily the end of the entertainment. If you stay until the early evening then you can experience the 'Night Extravaganza', fires are lit, the barbecue gets going and the heavy entertainment gets underway; often featuring djembe drumming, cultural dancing, acrobats, fire breathers, jugglers, stilted men (Mamapara). At the end of it all you are escorted out, dancing along a lantern lit procession between the trees before departing for your hotel.

Animals / Fauna:

Among the mammal species you might encounter in the various habitats are monkeys such as a troupe of Guinea Baboons, Western Red Colobus Monkeys, Vervet Monkeys. Other animals include the elusive mongoose, bats, squirrels and Dwarf deer. There are also reptiles such as monitor lizards and crocodiles along the riverbanks and in the water. Among the invertebrates are fiddler crabs, and insects such as termites and ants.

Birds / Avifauna:

Among the over 100 bird species birdwatching enthusiasts might see in Makasutu Cultural Forest are the Splendid Sunbird, African Paradise Flycatcher, Four-banded Sandgrouse, Little Bee-eater, Mouse-brown Sunbird, Blue-bellied Roller, Wattled Plover, Jacana, Western Reef Heron, Swallow-tailed Bee-eater, Red-cheeked Cordon-bleu, Red-billed Firefinch, Senegal thick-knee, Palm-nut Vulture, Great White Egret, Yellow-Billed Shrike, Violet Turaco, European Pied Wagtail, Senegal

Coucal, White-throated Bee-eater, Long-tailed Cormorant, Bearded Barbet, Red-billed Hornbill, Western Grey Plantain Eater, Laughing Dove, Lizard Buzzard, African Grey Hornbill, Black-crowned Tchagra, Yellow-fronted Tinkerbird, Speckled Pigeon, African Darter, Goliath Heron, Purple Heron, Blue-breasted Kingfisher and the Senegal Parrot.

Vegetation / Flora:

Among the vegetation in the woodland and wetland habitats are various palm trees such as coconuts, mangroves, silk cotton trees (kapok), banana, camel's foot tree, strangler figs, mahogany and baobab trees.

Health & Safety:

Before your visit to Makasutu Culture Forest consider carrying or wearing boots, thick trousers, a hat, UV sunglasses, a pocket torchlight, purified water, hand sanitizer, lip balm, a small rucksack, and rub on or spray plenty of mosquito repellent. Avoid turning over logs and stones due to the possible risk of being bitten by spiders or snakes, and don't swim in the creeks or river as there maybe crocodiles and other things around. If you have a modern mobile phone then carry it with you, along with a few phone numbers of members from your group, as well as your appointed tour guide. Download the Google maps app and find your location before your arrival, and learn how to use it. Finally, never wonder off alone.

Travel Information & How to Get There:

The best time of year to visit Makasutu is after the end of the Gambia's rainy season, between the end of November to April, when the grass is cleared from paths, visibility is best and animals congregate around ponds and streams. Independent travellers should take one of the bush taxis or 'Gelle Gelle' van from Serrekunda to Brikama, then get out and change to a taxi going to Kembujeh Village, however, it's a 3 kilometre walk from there. Alternatively, from Brikama you can take a 'town trip' (exclusive hire) to take you directly to the forest. The park also has a shuttle service departing from Brikama at about 9am and returning you at 4.30pm. The most convenient (and expensive) way to go is to simply hire a green jeep style 4x4 taxi for the time you want, from the Senegambia Strip taxi rank in Kololi. It will take you there and stay with you until you are ready to go back to your hotel. Expect to travel for 1 hour each way.

Travel to Sanyang

Introduction:

Sanyang Village and Sanyang Point beach resort are located in the Kombo South District in the West Coast Region in the southwest coastal area of The Gambia in West Africa. The old village is located 5km from the coast on the Kombo Coastal Road, and 31.54 km by road from capital of Banjul, and its estimated population of about 7,000 is comprised mostly of Mandinka, Wolof, Fula and Jola. The main economic activities here are farming and artisan fishing. There is a tarmac road that goes east from the centre of town, through Jambanjali (Jambanjelly) and Jalabang and onwards to the district capital of Brikama town.

Accommodation:

Not far from the holiday beach resort and just off the 'How Ba Road' is Kobokoto Lodge, with 20 rooms in huts and the main building, each with ensuite shower and WC. The Guesthouse Gambia has 3 double rooms and shared bathing and kitchen facilities. It has a pool, barbecue and four acres of garden. There is the Sanyang Nature Camp which has 32 African style round huts with ensuite shower, WC, bar and restaurant, and a big nature garden. On the beachfront is the Rainbow Lodge, with African style round huts, ensuite bathing, toilet and diner with bar.

Beach Area:

The 4.8km wide curve of finely grained Pelican, Osprey and Paradise Beach (jointly known as Sanyang Beach), were already drawing tourists to the area when the adjacent settlements were still far off the tourist trail. It is considered by many to be one of the best beachfronts in The Gambia, and which seems to have escaped much of the earlier coastal erosion. South of the fish centre the seafront is at its most remote and deserted, backed by inland lagoons fringed with mangroves.

About half a kilometre to your left is the fish landing site. The easiest way to get to the palm tree fringed sands is by the wide How Ba Road, which starts at the village crossroads and leads almost directly to the shore. To get to the vibrant coastal fishing centre you take the Sanyang Fishing Village Road which leads you through residential areas, farmland, scrubland, wooded areas, a mangrove fringed lagoon and onto the fish centre on the shore. This section has a bustling fish market where you can see small cold stores, women busy gutting and cleaning catches, crabs and seagulls picking at scraps, fishermen mending their nets, and dozens of colourful local and Senegalese pirogues.

Pirogues

During the tourist season and on Sundays throughout the year the main 'Paradise Beach' can get a little busy, but 250 metres further south it's a lot quieter. The strand has been described as "...a broad smooth sweep of firm sand backed by coconut palms..." (Rough Guide to West Africa, Trillo, 2008).

General Area:

At Sanyang Village you will find the alkalo's residence, and in the centre a taxi rank lined with tired looking Gambian 'Gelle Gelle' taxi vans, tyre repairers, street vendors, barbers, shops and the market's vegetable stalls. Concrete block houses with corrugated roofs dominate, and between them are sandy roads overlooked by huge mango trees providing residents with much needed shade. Along the high street is where Brikama Area Council have a collection office where you can make payments for your annual property rates. In 2006 villagers were grateful to be finally connected to the electricity grid, along with their own power station.

The best locations for nature and beach enthusiasts is between the main highway and the coast, in between is the sloping land area peppered with many hectares of woodland savanna with lofty 'koni' palms, cashew, baobab trees, casuarina, and further down are mangrove swamps, creeks, inland pools, dune swales and crop fields.

One of the earliest, large property developments in the region is the fenced, residential community at Aquasun Gardens with twelve, 3 bedroom, 2 storey villas with shared pool.

Founding Family History:
Oral history says that Sanyang Village was founded around 1918 by the Mandinka Bojang family, on what was mostly forested land. They were followed by other 'founding' families called Kore, Namba, Jabak and More Kunda who settled in nearby areas. The population continues to grow fairly rapidly as a result of migrants from southern Senegal, and people from the north west towns such as Serrekunda seeking to buy land on which to build houses.

Tourist Attractions & Things to Do:
Bird Watching

Sanyang is abundant in migratory and Gambian bird species due to its rich vegetation, variable habitat and wetlands. While birdwatching within the region you might be able to spot various raptors as well as African Paradise Flycatcher, Sanderling, Black Shouldered Kite, Turnstone, Hueglin's Masked Weavers, Ringed Plover, Bar Tail Godwit, African Palm Swift, Grey Plover and Whimbrel.

The lagoons and creeks are thriving with birds including, Spur Winged Plover, Grey Headed Gull,

Greenshank, Pied Kingfisher, Black Headed Heron, Caspian Tern, Ringed Plover, Cattle Egret, Lesser Black Back Gull, Long Tailed Cormorant and Intermediate Egret.

Sports Fishing

The best areas for angling are in the ocean and along the streams and lagoons close to the shore. To get to the inland waters just make your way to the fishing village on the shore; just before the main sheds to your left, is a wetland with mangroves where you can find Catfish. While sea fishing you can expect to catch Bobo, Longneck and Cassava Croaker, Snapper, Mackerel, Bonga, Sunpat Grunt, Stingray, Butterfish, Captain Fish and Guitarfish. Going further out to sea by boat it's possible to catch Tarpon.

Sanyang Fish Market

FishermenAt times a hectic spot where you will see up close vibrantly coloured Gambian pirogues parked on the shore. The air is full of the smell of fish and sea snails, and hoards of flies make their way from fish pile to fish pile, while men pull the heavy wooden pirogues onto shore. The market has three stores, as well as a special vegetable and meat market. Smoking, chilling and salting is carried out in the curing sheds at the rear. While there you can buy some unfrozen, fresh fish and sometimes crabs, lobsters and 'edible' sea snails (Cymbium).

Nature Treks

With its well shaded footpaths and varying habitats there is plenty of wildlife, scrub and trees in the area.

Beach Bars & Restaurants

During the winter holiday season you are likely to see a number of juice bar stalls dotted along the sands catering mostly to tourists. Most of the coastal bars in Sanyang were demolished in 2013 by orders of the Gambian authorities.

Black and White
Freeman's Place
Marcus's Beer Garden
Rainbow Bar
Osprey Beach Bar & Restaurant
Sanyang International Cultural Festival

Held each January, the first event was held between the 24th to 27th January, 2013, which had amongst its performers was the Kora player Jaliba Kuyateh. The festival is 4 days of contemporary and traditional world music, cultural dance, a tourism fair, African cuisine, kid's games, arts and crafts, visiting historic places and sacred shrines. Some of the money generated goes to helping poor school children and improving school facilities.

Health & Safety:

The area is more remote than the Gambia's other resorts north of Tanji and there is a lot of wilderness here. Daytime is fairly safe but at night do not go out unaccompanied. Use a vehicle in the evening if possible, otherwise stay close to your lodgings at night. Also carry your mobile phone and a pocket torch.

Travel Information:

To get to Sanyang Village take one of the green tourist taxis at Banjul Airport and head southeast towards Brusubi. At Brusubi turn left and continue past Tanji, Batokunku, Tujering and other settlements until you get to the village junction. The other route is from the airport go south to Brikama, then directly west into the settlement's centre. See if your accommodation offers airport transfers as this is most advised.

Travel to Serrekunda

Introduction:

The former village of Serrekunda market town (also spelt Serekunda) is the Gambia's largest town, and its name means the 'home of the Sayer family' (Sayer Kunda), named after its 19th century founder, Sayerr Jobe, a Wolof royal from Koki, Senegal. Serrekunda has a population of about 390,000, and is 13km to the southwest of the capital, Banjul. It is actually made up of nine villages which have merged into an urban sprawl, that incorporates the villages of Latrikunda, Dippa Kunda, Bundung and London Corner, and effectively forms the Kanifing LGA, in the Kombo St. Mary District. The urban settlement is about 3 kilometres inland from the coastal resorts of Kololi and Kotu.

Accommodation:

Serrekunda Town is not an obvious holiday resort destination for tourists visiting The Gambia. Most visitors head out from Banjul Airport and straight to the beach resorts, and check-in to hotels in Kololi / Senegambia, Kotu, Bijilo, Brufut, Fajara, Kerr Sering, Cape Point and other Atlantic Ocean coastal lodges. However, there are a few simple, basic types of hotels in Serrekunda providing minimal amenities and some with air-conditioning.

Tourist Attractions & Things to Do

Serrekunda Market

The Gambia's commercial centre and heart of the town is said to have been originally started by several women regularly setting up their stalls by a dirt path selling a few fresh vegetables and dried fish. As time went by other local food sellers joined them and it subsequently grew into the bustling market it is today. It has now effectively spread out to encompass nearly all the nearby roads leading into the market area and many of their side streets. Pavements merge into the road with pedestrians dominating half the road on either side, letting vehicles through occasionally.

If you want to get a good feel of day-to-day, urban West African cultural existence; a trip to the core of town Market buildingoffers you a strong experience. At times the centre's major roads are filled with bumper-to-bumper vehicles, spewing out diesel fumes, taxis repeatedly blaring their horns, loud music played from any number of ghetto blasters and radios, and streets thronging with over-full colourful stands, wheelbarrow boys pushing heavy goods for their clients, street hawkers and traders' stores selling a jumble of cheap imports. Goods literally spill out of their shop fronts in an organised or de-organised way.

Inside the market building is a labyrinth of workshops, trading stalls and eateries which fills up the Serrekunda Market building. Inside the main structure the stands are demarcated by small alleys. This is the sort of jammed-to-the-hilt location where you can find an endless stream of products, from bicycle repair kits and flip-flops to flowery vases, ceramic trade beads, bed sheets and pillows. There's also a large outdoor food selling area at the back, where mostly women offer vegetables like hot chillies, tomatoes, green peppers, salad as well ad dried and smoked bonga (shad), fresh fish, smoked catfish from wooden stalls, mounds on the floor or on decorated metal bowls. Adjacent stores sell all manner of dried and packaged foods such as groundnut paste, rice, cooking oil, herbs, spices, dried chillies, Maggie cubes and much more.

Note: It is illegal to export any article made from wild animal skins, feathers or any other part of any protected creature from The Gambia. Offenders will have the products confiscated and fines may be imposed .

Serrekunda Town

The main artery leading southwest towards the market is the Sayerr Jobe Avenue, which is jammed with local shops, ageing taxis, handicraft sellers, street peddlers and wholesale merchants' stores, from all over West Africa and several Arab countries.

Walking and shopping along Sayer Jobe Avenue is usually enough for anybody. Close to the enclosed market at the corner of Sayerr Jobe Avenue and Mosque Road, every metre of road-side is often taken by traders and shoppers, and every section of road is blocked with autos, barrows, cyclists, motorbikes and even more pedestrians!

Main Serrekunda MarketBeyond the immediate market vicinity, the busy commercial roads offer up interesting perusing and shopping possibilities, with a large variety of commodities on display. You'll pass photo studios, barbers, fabrics shops selling tailoring ribbons, bobbins, headscarves, textiles and lace, people selling any number of unrecognisable dried leaves, twigs, bark and powders, plastic utensils are everywhere, iron mongers' workshops, with rows of strung aluminium ladles, incense burners, and neat stacks of large, shiny, aluminium cooking pots on protruding legs and iron cooking stoves. You can also find carpenters working from cramped workshops, chiselling and carving ornate wooden beds, wardrobes and other local furniture.

Batik Factory

For tie-dyed and batik fabrics, Serrekunda has a well known "Batik Factory", Ms. Musu Kebba Drammeh's workshop in Dippa Kunda, off the Mosque Road. On the 10th March, 2003, Musu Kebba passed away and the management of the workshop passed onto her daughter. You are not usually allowed to observe craftspeople at work here, but if you are lucky, you might see the tie dye and batik making process from the design, waxing and boiling, to the finished material. Use the opportunity to get hold of some souvenirs. There are lots of finished fabrics for sale, including clothing and wall coverings, plus a stand selling wood carvings such as masks and djembe drums.

Wrestling

This is the national sport of the Senegambia region. Wrestling contests usually take place on Saturdays and Sundays in the local wrestling arenas such as in the Serrekunda West Mini Stadium, or at the National Stadium in Bakau. Each wrestler has a group of djembe drummers who rhythmically, and vigorously beat their drums and blow pea-whistles before each bout. The winner of each bout is the one who gets his opponent on the ground first. Kicking, punching, biting, and throwing sand into an opponent's face are not against the rules, but is frowned upon, and the referee or the offender's manager could step in and stop the bout. Spectators would normally make their disapproval clear by booing.

Paper Recycling Skills Project

One place worth visiting is the Paper Recycling Skills Project (PRSP) in Fajikunda. You can buy various paper products; and any profits generated goes back into the community. PRSP is located a little further south of Serrekunda's centre, in the 'Craft Village', in Fajikunda, near Latrikunda. It was founded in 2001 by May Rooney, an English artist, to create job opportunities and training, support education projects and encourage a recycling culture in The Gambia, the project produces attractive, handmade paper, school exercise books and covers, cards, albums and lampshades and more from discarded materials. Profit is used to buy school equipment and other community items. In early 2012 the charity launched a biomass recycling research and training centre at Fajikunda–Abuko. It involves creating doughnut briquettes made from waste paper and waste agricultural materials to be used as an alternative fuel in cooking stoves. This was set up to support the local community in enhancing their capacity to better preserve and protect the country's forest areas.

Kairaba Avenue

Formerly known as the Pipeline Road, it links the genteel Fajara residential section and Serrekunda. In the 1970s it was essentially a rough dirt road coursing through fields and past a few built homes. Today, the 1.86 mile length of Kairaba Avenue is straddled by food stores, supermarkets, banks, office blocks, restaurants, electronic shops, furniture stores etc., and attracts the steepest rents in The Gambia. It joins the Banjul to Brikama highway at the busy Westfield Junction roundabout.

Towards the southern end of the avenue is a tall, modern building of a mobile phone operator's head office, Latrikunda Upper Basic School, many retail stores and next to the football playing field is the area's main cultural centre, the Alliance Franco-Gambienne (or Alliance Française). The French Cultural Centre is focused on teaching French classes, cultural activities such as theatre and live musical performances and French and English film viewings. There is a library, a cafeteria and a music recording studio which local talent can hire and record their own music.

Mosque Road & Latrikunda

If you go down Mosque Road from Latrikunda German from Kairaba Avenue, you should be able to spot the 'Big Tree'; a revered and genuinely huge silk cotton tree, just clipping the main road. Most of this end of Mosque Road is often nicely shaded with trees and an interesting place to wonder down. The commercial buzz becomes increasingly hectic as you stroll south towards Dippa Kunda and the main commercial district.

Night Clubs

Serrekunda is an ideal place to get a sampling of local nightlife, and it's home to The Gambia's well established Jokor Nightclub. It is a fairly safe place for tourists to visit as it is on the well lit Westfield Junction / Kombo Sillah Drive, and has a moderate crowd with fairly decent guest facilities such as toilets. There is also plenty of car parking space available around the back, which is guarded. The revelling doesn't really get going much before 12am; then goes on until 4am or later, when club goers move on in search of a fast food meal, very often afra.

Restaurants

While Serrekunda's restaurants are not geared towards tourists, it has some good local eating establishments, particularly near the market. A good place to visit for some quick food and a break is Sen Fast Food on Sayerr Jobe Avenue and near Westfield Junction or Four Seasons which is further west on Kairaba Avenue. There are some local bars in town which get busy at night; many of these occasionally see travellers, and you'll almost certainly be welcome. Try to keep to the ones on the main street or not too far.

Health & Safety:

Pickpockets are quite active in the crowded sections, so keep your cash, jewellery and credit cards well tucked away in a money belt or bum bag. In the evening this urban area might seem like a menacing town to the inexperienced; and it makes no special provisions for tourists' safety. In reality, however, there's not much to be afraid of in terms of crime, especially if you're with Gambian friends. Avoid walking in unlit areas alone at night and always carry a small torchlight. Do not use the light on your mobile phone as it could get snatched and never walk alone after 12pm. The police station is only a stones throw from the busy market junction and normally well lit at night. There is also a fire station.

Travel Information:

To get into the centre of Serrekunda from the Gambia's coastal resorts like Kololi and Kotu you take one of the yellow or green tourist taxis and ask to be taken to the market. If you just say Serrekunda you could end up being dropped quite a distance from the centre as it is now an urban agglomeration, taking in several villages in the process. If you want to shop and enjoy a stroll while making your way up to the main market, then ask to be taken to Westfield Junction and walk up Sayerr Jobe Avenue. You can also ask to be dropped off near the former 'Tipper Garage' in Bakoteh, and make your way from there.

To get back to your accommodation just pick up a cheaper yellow cab and ask them to take you to your lodgings. Most drivers know all the main hotels and lodges, and your taxi fare shouldn't cost you more than the equivalent of £2.50.

Travel to Tanji Village

Introduction:
Tanji Village (also spelt Tanjeh or Tanje), often called the Tanji Fishing Village, is close to the Atlantic Ocean beach, in the northern section of the Kombo South District, West Coast Region of The Gambia, in West Africa. The settlement is 30km by road from the capital of Banjul, and approximately 12km southwest of Kololi resort, and adjacent to the Kombo Coastal Road. The main ethnic groups are Mandinka, Wolof, Jola, and Serer, the last group are traditionally the fisherfolk, while the former are generally engaged in farming, crafts and petty

trading. The village centre is located about 1km from the main fishing bay.

Accommodation:

There are just a few places to stay in Tanji. Among them are the Nyanya's Beach Lodge, which is located on the shore and the river estuary, and lies next to the fisheries centre. It has a small beach and its main entrance is on the main road. There is also the Kairoh Garden Guest House, which has 18 modern, Gambian style rows of rooms, clean and simply furnished, 10 with ensuite shower room, sink and WC.

Beach Area:

There are basically two types of beaches in Tanji. The first is directly in front of the fishing village and is a fish landing site, so it is not suitable for swimming or sunbathing. Because it's a very active, working beach, you'll find it scattered with old, shredded gillnets, sea snail shells, malodorous rotting seafood, plastic bags and bottles, and other flotsam and jetsam, floating on the water or resting on the shore. The air is filled with the odour of smoked fish; an unimaginable number of flies swarm around fresh or discarded seafood, seagulls hover overhead looking for scraps, fishermen land their afternoon catch from long African pirogues, passing buckets of catch onto the heads of local women, who then ferry it to the shore. Activity is frenzied and messy, but surprisingly efficient.

To the north of Tanji fishing village, after the bridge, is the Karinti Bird Reserve, where the coastline has a few sand bars and lagoons, where the beach is far cleaner and relatively deserted, but access is often hindered by dense, scrub woodland. About 1km south of the fishing village, the bay's strand is more of what you would expect as holiday standard; clean, white sands, backed by a strip of palms and shoreline scrub. You will see the occasional passerby or meandering herd of cows.

General Area:
To the north of the main settlement the area is characterised by riverine mangroves of the Tanji River, sand banks, salt-flats lagoons, lily pools, dry woodland, and coastal dune scrub. To the south of the river are residential compounds, interspersed with trees, farmland, shoreline fisheries structures, and strand. The village's main road leads inland from the main freeway, which itself passes close to the Atlantic Ocean, just south of the small, mangrove-fringed river.

Tourist Attractions & Things To Do:
Camel Riding

Pepe's is a long established operation which was started from the compound of the Spanish Captain of the tour boat, M/V Joven Antonio. Pepe's Tanji Camel Safaris offers guided camel rides along the beach to tourists, with each dromedary carrying up to two riders for half or one hour, and you finish off with a beach barbecue and drinks. There are a few restrictions on those allowed to ride such as children below 8, and people with bodily complaints.

Village Museum

The privately run Tanji Village Museum is made up of grass thatched mud huts that hold the exhibits of ethnographic artifacts, such as traditional musical instruments, and antique furniture. The displays are labelled with helpful accompanying descriptions of each. There is also a photo gallery section on various birds, fish, Gambian plant species and their medicinal properties, as well as local history and culture. Visitors can also chat and intermingle with the various craftsmen working at their stations. There is also a nature track and a handicrafts area, plus a restaurant cooking up some European cuisine and traditional Gambian food and drink. The museum sometimes puts on live music and cultural dance performances in their garden Bantaba (shaded area). There is also guest accommodation provided, a shop selling selling DVDs, fabrics, jewellery and paintings,

67302012R00105

a conference room with a capacity of about 40 people, and a traditional Mandinka family hamlet on display.

Bird Watching

Going north, at the start of the bridge is the Karinti Bird Reserve, whose southern boundary encloses the tidal, saline reaches of the small Tanji River, and encompasses the Bald Cape promontory, and the Bijol Islands (Kajonyi), which itself is situated almost 1 mile from the Atlantic Ocean shoreline. Together, both areas provide a broad range of superb habitats for birdwatching, such as lagoons, riverine, sandbanks, salt-flats, mangrove and coastal scrub. Among the Palearctic migratory and resident bird species you can find here are waders, raptors and seabirds such as White Straight Crested Helmetshrike, Ruddy Turnstone, Sandwich Terns, Subalpine Warblers, Dominican Gulls, White-fronted Plovers, Palm-nut Vultures, Whistling Cisticolas, Common Nightingales, Northern Crombecs, Pelicans, Yellow-crowned Gonoleks and Four-banded Sand Grouse. On Bijol Islands you might be able to spot, among other species, Western Reef Herons, Royal Terns and Grey-headed Caspian Terns.

Wildlife Spotting

Within the locality of Bijol Islands are reptiles, invertebrates and mammals, such as minke whales, bottle-nose dolphins, fiddler crabs, green turtles, birds, upside down jelly fish, sand crabs, ghost crabs, mud skippers, Atlantic Humpback Dolphins, bushbuck, Clawless otter, Senegal bushbaby, and Gambian mongoose. Access to the island itself is restricted to research purposes only. On the mainland side of the reserve you might spot Patas Monkeys, Porcupines, Bushbucks, Western Red Colobus Monkeys and other animals.

Tanji Community Fisheries Centre

The harbour was upgraded and finally inaugurated in 2001. The centre is one of the seven major coastal artisanal fishing communities in the Gambia, and is at the centre of the local economy. It was developed with grant-in-aid to the tune of US$ 4.5 million from the Japanese government. Among the facilities here are an ice-plant, chill room, refrigerated trucks, smoking houses, fishmonger's sales area. Three dozen or so people are directly employed here, with a further 2,000 people engaged in activities linked to the fishing village. The species which are most often smoked are Shads, marine Catfish, Barracuda, Sharks and round and flat Sardinella spp. Eighty percent of the landings consists of Bonga (shad); 40% of which are preserved by smoking. The curing with firewood

is done by hired men and a portion of the smoked fish is exported to neighbouring West African countries like Nigeria, Ghana and Senegal. In view of the huge quantities of shad caught here, Tanji has long been called the 'Bonga Capital of The Gambia'.

The most prominent features of the fishing market are its dim, shad smoking sheds, lines of majestic African pirogues parked onshore - decorated in bright geometric shapes, hired hands and housewives lining the shore, waiting for the afternoon catch, fishmongers and customers haggling over prices, wheelbarrow boys with mounds of fish and women making a living as carriers of buckets of the fishermen's' catch. You can try and visit one of the curing sheds, and watch the preservation process, amid the smoke and pungent kipper like aroma. There is a small general market incorporated into the seaside town selling plastic bags, bowls and other small goods. Bargain hunters regularly visit the site as the seafood sold here is generally cheaper here than those in the inland markets of the Kombos.

Restaurants & Beach Bars

Nyanya's Beach Lodge +220 4414021

Village Museum +220 992 6618

Kairoh Garden +220 9903526

Health & Safety:

Tanji is in a rural area of The Gambia, so you need to take care regarding going alone at night into unfamiliar territory. All the major health facilities are some distance from here, so you need to be vigilant with regards to your health. Don't drink the water straight from the tap in the village, as it may be contaminated; instead you can use a water filter, or boil the water first. Protect yourself against insect bites and stings, and only wear thick trousers and boots when venturing into areas of high vegetation; this is to avoid any nasty surprises from spiders and other harmful creatures.

Travel Information:

To get to Tanji fishing village you can take a taxi van from Serrekunda, which comes directly to the rural community, with no getting off in between. From Kololi or Kotu you can also make your way along the Kombo Coastal Road to Brusubi, then change for one of the taxis going southwest to the settlement.

Art and Culture

Gambian arts and culture is characterized by heterogeneity and diversity. As Gambia subscribes to most of the UNESCO culture conventions, our activities continue to be guided by the spirit of these Conventions which call for the safeguard and development of both the tangible and intangible aspects of cultural heritage, including the arts, for a more peaceful world. We are particularly keen on utilizing our cultural diversity as a source of strength, to galvanize our people to common understanding and mutual respect of each other's values and traditions. Hence our support of festivals as a means to achieving this end.

In the realm of material heritage we are most proud of our UNESCO World Heritage Listings, Kunta Kinteh Island and Related Sites (2003) and the Stone Circles of the Senegambia (2006), testimony to the outstanding universal significance of these sites. Our

National Museums continue to increase, serving as not only repositories for representative samples of the movable aspects of our cultural patrimony, but centres for study and cultural motivation.

We will continue to strive to attain international recognition for our intangible cultural heritage, which reached a milestone with the proclamation of the Kankurang as 'Masterpiece of the Oral and Intangible Heritage of Humanity in 2005 by UNESCO. Our next target is the inscription of our invaluable oral archives in the UNESCO Memory of the World Register.

Since 2004 copyright administration has also come under the purview of the NCAC. A copyright office has been established under the NCAC and charged with sensitization registration and enforcement. The Board of the Collecting Society of The Gambia, mandated under the Copyright Act, 2004, has also been inaugurated. We are currently working with all stakeholders to ensure implementation of an effective copyright regime in the short to medium term.

Culture must be seen as an integral part of our national development efforts. It is only through the recognition of the cultural dimension of development that our country can chart a course of

development that will meet the needs and aspirations of The Gambian people.

This revamped NCAC website serves to once again introduce our services and the resources at our disposal. It will also endeavour to give regular updates on our activities and the cultural milieu in The Gambia. I enjoin all who visit the site to provide us feedback, and ask questions through the portal which will be regularly updated.

Acknowledgments

We express gratitude to individuals and colleagues who gave out their time in search of information to make this book a reality, which we have successfully achieved. These individuals are AMELIA ACKER, JACK ASH, and JOSEPH BOLT of **Digital Light Publishing.**

We will be updating you with the information on in further edition of this book Gambia Travel and Tourism in all field, when due.